BROKEN CITY

CHRIS HARRIS AND MARY JANE WALKER

First published in 2024 by A Maverick Traveller Ltd.
P O Box 44 146, Point Chevalier, Auckland 1246
www.a-maverick.com

© 2024 Christopher E. Harris and Mary Jane Walker

All rights reserved. Except for the purpose of fair reviewing, no part of this publication may be reproduced or transmitted in any form or by any means, electronic or mechanical, including photocopying, recording or any information storage and retrieval system, without prior written permission from the publisher.

ISBN: 978-0-473-73635-4 (paperback), 978-0-473-73636-1 (Kindle)

Disclaimer

Although the authors and publisher have made every effort to ensure that the information in this book was correct at the time of publication, the author and publisher do not assume and hereby disclaim any liability to any party for any loss, damage, or disruption caused by errors or omissions, whether such errors or omissions result from negligence, accident, or any other cause.

Fonts

The font used on the front cover and spine is Impact, and in the front matter, a mixture of Calibri and Garamond.

The interior text of the print version is typeset in Calibri throughout.

Cover Artwork

The cover artwork includes a colourised image of the Grafton area of Auckland in 1949 which also appears in the body of the work (Whites Aviation Collection image WA-19229-F. Alexander Turnbull Library, Wellington, New Zealand. /records/22512926) and the Wikimedia Commons files

'Auckland_City_Of_Sails_(1236307630).jpg' by 'Sids1,' dated 26 August 2007, CC BY 2.0, and 'Rangitoto_Island_North_Head.jpg' by Ingolfson, dated 12 February 2007, a public domain image.

Colour Images and Author Details

All images in the interior of this book can be seen free of charge, and in colour where they are already in colour, in a summary blog post called 'Broken City' that appears in substantially identical form on the following URLs:

https://medium.com/a-maverick-traveller/broken-city-c5ef89992e23

https://medium.com/@chris-harris/broken-city-ce990d20192e

https://www.a-maverick.com/blog/broken-city

These are on the Medium [dot] com postings of Mary Jane Walker and Chris Harris and the blog of Mary Jane Walker, respectively.

Chris Harris is a former Chairperson of the Mount Albert Community Board, in Auckland, and holds a PhD in planning. Dr Harris can be contacted on suburbanosis [at] gmail [dot] com.

Mary Jane Walker is a former Auckland City Councillor who holds an MA in political studies. Ms Walker can be contacted on admin [at] a-maverick[dot] com.

CHRIS HARRIS AND MARY JANE WALKER

Contents

Introduction: 'Auckland! You Poor Bastard' 1

Auckland as it Might Have Been 15

'An Account of Missed Chances' 25

Wellington on the Waitematā: Further Reflections on Auckland as it Might Have Been 41

Countryfied 59

Our Forgotten Land Banks 67

Getting Back on Track 77

The Light Rail Saga 95

Conclusion: No More Missed Chances? 103

CHRIS HARRIS AND MARY JANE WALKER

Introduction: 'Auckland! You Poor Bastard'

JUST lately, the Minister of Transport, Simeon Brown, and Wayne Brown announced that responsibility for planning transport in Auckland is to be placed under the control of a refounded Regional Land Transport Committee.

This might be seen to hand responsibility for transport planning to the city and its politicians from Auckland Transport, except that central government will **still get to pick the committee's chair and most of its members.**

The Minister of Transport also intervened to raise Auckland's inner city speed limits, claiming that an international road safety award for lowering them was a "woke" award.

It seems odd that Auckland isn't trusted to have full responsibility for its own planning. After all, the population of Auckland today is about the same as that of New Zealand as a whole in the World War II era.

That our greatest city is looked upon so negatively and with mistrust is a striking feature of life in New Zealand.

Introduction: 'Auckland! You poor bastard.'

A few years ago, Bill Ralston had a regular column in the *New Zealand Listener*. In the issue of 10 November 2007, he wrote about a colleague's transfer to Auckland, as follows:

> *"Auckland! You poor bastard," they cried in unison, and shouted him a beer.*

And yet Auckland—or should we say Tāmaki-makau-rau, Tāmaki of a hundred lovers, Tāmaki desired by many—is in a lovely place to build a city and always was, with its strategic harbours and terraced green volcanoes, most of them once with a pā on top.

> *Today is one of Auckland's ravishing days of exquisite beauty, enough to make a man foreswear heaven & worship the beauty of the lower earth.*

Thus wrote the modern city's most famous founder, as quoted in R. C. J. Stone, *The Father and his Gift: John Logan Campbell's Later Years* (1987). "Last, loneliest, loveliest, exquisite—apart" was Kipling's more famous judgement.

Many early buildings, structures, and parks added to the city's beauty: the art deco libraries of Parnell, Grey Lynn, and Remuera, the Art Gallery, the Civic, St James and His Majesty's theatres, the Auckland Domain, the Winter Gardens, the War Memorial Museum, Devonport, Cheltenham, the Savage Memorial, Takapuna and Mission Bay Beaches, the old university buildings, Grafton Bridge, the Scarborough and

Alberon Reserves, and St Andrew's, St Mary's, St Patrick's and St-Matthew-in-the-City.

To these we may add the extraordinary old-time yachting photographs that put Auckland on the map as the 'City of Sails' (see 'Kiwis Shine at the Jewel City'), and such social firsts as Elizabeth Yates, the first woman in the British Empire, as it then was, to be elected mayor, of Onehunga in 1893.

These are just a few of our favourite things to tell visitors about.

Yet the city has since declined into ugliness, congestion, and unaffordability.

When he was the editor of the local magazine Metro, Simon Wilson wrote, in the April 2009 issue, that:

> *In Auckland there's a gap. On the one hand the natural attractions and the magnificent early efforts of the city fathers; on the other, the paucity of the whole post-war built environment. This gap is so huge, everyone responsible should hang their heads in shame.*

(The story from which that quote comes, 'The City's Shame: Why Is Auckland's Urban Design So Bad?', was republished in 2015 and is accessible online.)

There is a simple reason for this decline, and this is that Auckland has grown many times larger since 1945, in ways that have not been provided for.

In 1945, the population of Auckland, its suburbs (then independent) and its outlying satellite towns was around 250,000. It was a population served by trams, ferries, trains, and bicycles, plus the occasional automobile.

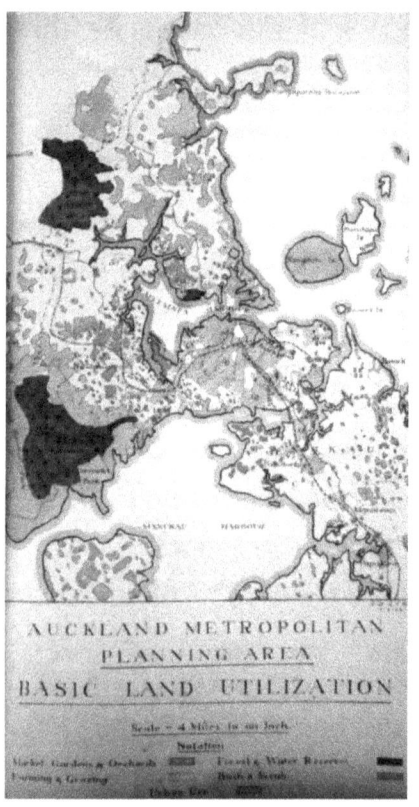

From the Outline Development Plan for Auckland *(1949 version), Auckland Metropolitan Planning Organisation, held currently in the Auckland Council Archives (AMO 002/3). North at top. Reproduced with the permission of Auckland Council.*

But if we fast-forward to the present, Auckland now has a population of 1.7 million and a much more sprawling, congested, and car-dependent form than it had in 1945.

ISS True-colour photograph of Auckland, NZ, September 2015. Image courtesy of the Earth Science and Remote Sensing Unit, NASA Johnson Space Center. NASA Photo ID ISS045-E-33579 taken 25 September 2015 at 22:36:50 GMT. North is somewhere to the top right.

'Distant and Separate'

Auckland's growth was nearly always underestimated and lowballed by officials and politicians who, bluntly, did not wish to spend the money needed to provide for so much future growth at one end of the country.

An end of the country that, moreover, seemed distant and remote to the majority of New Zealanders, who dwelt not just south of the Bombay Hills but south of Taupō and its volcanic wilderness.

A colonial writer, Mrs Eliza Wilson, noted in an 1894 book called *In the Land of the Tui* that "Wellington, Christchurch and Dunedin are always *en rapport,* but Auckland appears distant and separate."

In a 1977 essay collection called *Auckland at Full Stretch*-- published, ironically enough, when Auckland had about half its present population—the historian Keith Sinclair added that "Frank Sargeson once said that the dividing line in New Zealand is not Cook Strait but at Taupō. It is true. . . ."

And Auckland is not just geographically estranged from what we might call South Zealand. It is also far more multicultural, far less overwhelmingly Pākehā.

Before it began to be called Auckland, the site of the future city was already Tāmaki-makau-rau: Tāmaki desired by many. Tāmaki-makau-rau was the largest concentration of Pā and stonefields agriculture in the country, a sort of proto-city already, a future Tenochtitlán had the Māori been left to their own devices and its terraced volcanoes terraced some more, perhaps.

'Such is Auckland Now'

But the Māori of Tāmaki-makau-rau would not be left to their own devices: the site of the city being acquired, instead, in the time of Governor Hobson and thereafter, for what now seems a peppercorn consideration. In the words of Hamish Keith, OBE, narrator of a 1971 documentary called 'Auckland City Centenary',

> ... Hobson came, and for fifty blankets, fifty pounds of money, twenty trousers, twenty shirts, ten waistcoats, ten caps, four casks of tobacco, one box of pipes, a hundred yards of gown pieces, ten iron pots, one bag of sugar, one bag of flour, and twenty hatchets, he bought three thousand acres of the Waitematā.
>
> A year later, at something like fourpence an acre, another thirteen thousand acres were added.

For more on those days, check out Wayne Thompson's 2003 *New Zealand Herald* article 'Shady Deals Laid City Foundations'.

Māori living in the Waikato traded with Auckland and with Australia, using the Waikato River, which is navigable all the way to Cambridge, as a highway. Ironically, the success of Māori enterprise in the Waikato led to covetous eyes being cast on its lands.

Further dispossession followed in the wars of the 1860s: wars that were themselves mostly fought in South Auckland and the Waikato.

In a book called *The Big Smoke,* the late urban scholar Ben Schrader included a quote, with original emphasis, from a 5 November 1863 letter by a soldier named Fred Haslam, who was guarding a fort at Drury, now an industrial suburban of Auckland. In the letter, Haslam complained that:

> *The once happy New Zealand, a land of homesteads and farms, cattle, and rosy children playing on the green meadows, is now the scene of ruin, desolation and bloodshed of the most barbarous character, and, worse than all, the destruction is* by our own defenders, *the lawless mob introduced from Australia. . . . What fearful scenes I have witnessed of late, years of toil destroyed by Maoris & defenders while the inhabitants are out defending another part. Such is Auckland now. (p. 179)*

The Queen City

For the best part of a century or so, thereafter, the city was overwhelmingly Pākehā with small minorities of Indian and Chinese merchants and market gardeners, working in a fertile hinterland in which such varieties as Albany Surprise grapes, Mangere ryegrass and Oratia Beauty apples were cultivated.

Plus a few Māori still, notably at Ōrākei (where the marae was burned in 1951), until the Māori began to return in earnest, in ways that were soon joined by Pasifika migrants.

Although there was some anti-immigrant tension and little official recognition of Māori culture in those days, jobs were plentiful, and houses were cheap.

In his history of twentieth-century New Zealand, *Paradise Reforged*, James Belich has gone so far as to describe the three decades after World War II as a "golden age" for Māori in economic terms, the income and homeownership gap between Pākehā and urbanised Māori narrowing to just ten per cent or so. (p. 474)

The early part of this period, at least, was the golden age of Auckland in physical terms as well: its heyday as the Queen City of the South Pacific, not yet despoiled by motorways, as we can see from the 1949 aerial photograph on the next page. A photo that shows the Auckland Domain, Auckland's oldest park, designated in 1844 on the site known in Māori as Pukekawa ('bitter hill'), to the left, and Grafton Gully to the east beneath Grafton Bridge, a rare example of pre-World-War-One reinforced-concrete architecture.

Both the Domain and Grafton Bridge are of international renown, while Grafton Gully was long regarded as a beauty spot through which city workers could stroll through remnants of lowland native bush to the Domain.

Introduction: 'Auckland! You poor bastard.'

The Auckland Domain, Grafton Gully and Grafton Bridge on 29 January 1949. Source: 'Grafton Road, Auckland', Whites Aviation Ltd: Photographs. Ref: WA-19229-F. Alexander Turnbull Library, Wellington, New Zealand. /records/22512926. Much of this area is now beneath Auckland's obtrusive Central Motorway Junction, aka 'Spaghetti Junction'. Colourised by Palette.

But that was then, and this is now. There's a motorway through Grafton Gully now, a motorway that kept on being enlarged right through into the 1980s if not beyond.

Many Māori who had initially migrated the inner city from rural districts to which their ancestors had been displaced in the time of the colonial-era New Zealand Wars, and inner-city

Pasifika lately arrived from the islands of the South Pacific, were displaced to West and South Auckland in the 1960s and 1970s.

A planning map from 1968, overleaf, describes how there was already pressure, at that time, to disperse the large inner-city minority community, even if the means were as yet unspecified.

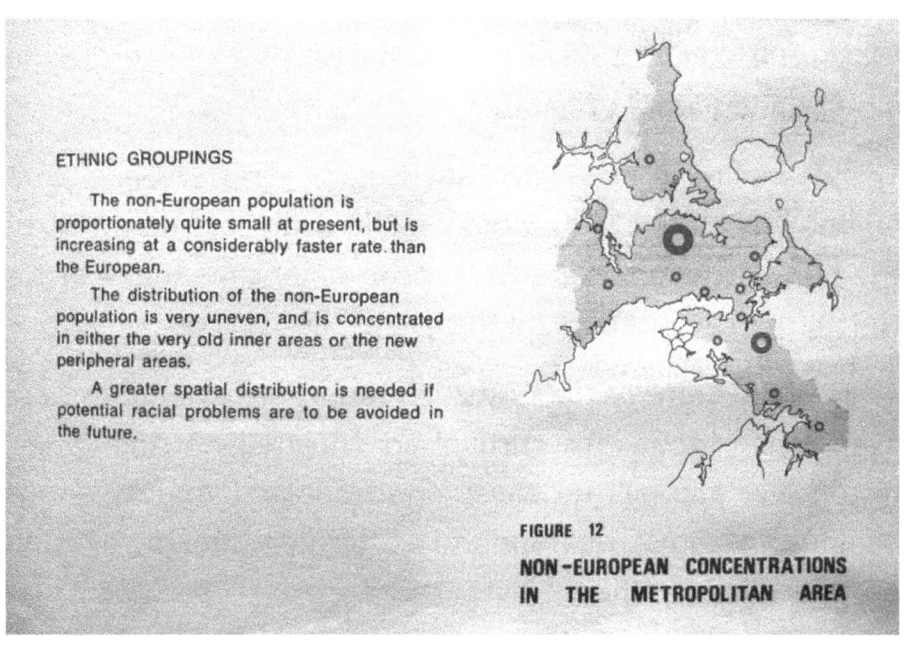

From *Development in the Auckland Region* (Auckland Regional Authority, 1968). Crown Copyright reserved.

It is thus perhaps no coincidence that the inner-city immigration crackdown known as the Dawn Raids and the development of Auckland's Central Motorway Junction happened in the same era.

Tensions, and poverty, have also gradually increased since those times. In the face of forty years of economic restructuring and exploding house prices, Māori homeownership in Auckland has plummeted from over 50%, in 1986 according to the 2020 Ngāi Tahu Reearch Centre report *The Impact of Housing Policy on Māori in Tāmaki Makaurau*, to just 18% as of the latest census, a figure given in Auckland's *State of the City 2023 report*.

This is really a five-alarm sociological fire, given that a homeownership rate of 18% is significantly less than half of the homeownership rate for African-Americans today or for Northern Irish Catholics on the eve of the Troubles.

And, as the *State of the City 2023* report also mentions, less even than that for urbanised Australian Aborigines, historically among the most disadvantaged of indigenous peoples, victims of numerous frontier massacres and protected by no official treaty.

In Auckland, it is as if the Treaty of Waitangi did not exist.

In his 2009 Auckland-noir novel *Cut and Run,* Greg McGee, writing as Alix Bosco, included the following passage:

> *I once saw a woman, now living in Australia, who told the television interviewer that she'd left New Zealand because*

she thought it was 'about to explode'. She wasn't talking about volcanoes: she'd been a social worker in South Auckland. (pp. 27–28)

That was fifteen years ago. It hasn't happened yet, but by the same token that does not mean it never could, especially when one thinks of the repeated indigenous dispossession that seems to be a *leitmotiv* of Auckland history.

In the remainder of this book, we will make a deeper dive into how Auckland fell into its current chaos, and what we can do to recover the city's promise.

Introduction: 'Auckland! You poor bastard.'

Chapter 1

Auckland as it Might Have Been

I DO ask you to be careful of these planners, said the head of the Auckland Regional Authority Transport Committee, Councillor J. Alsopp-Smith, to the 1969 Auckland Rapid Rail Symposium, "because if we are not careful they'll have to plan another change. They'll have to plan that the name of this fair city is changed from Auckland to Talkland."

In this chapter, we'll be talking about how Auckland has for so long been a day late and a dollar short when it comes to planning and investing, for its growth.

Growth that, since Cr. Alsopp-Smith's day if not longer, seems to have taken Auckland, and still more so the rest of New Zealand, as an unwelcome surprise.

For more than half a century, everything really bold has been kicked for touch in Auckland. Or at best, only built decades after the need for it had become obvious.

Ideas permanently kicked for touch have included a plan, aired at the same symposium, whereby we would have beaten future congestion by channeling Auckland's future growth onto four corridors kept free of congestion by progressively improving their public transport up to the level of fast, electrified rapid rail: the so-called Multi-Linear Scheme.

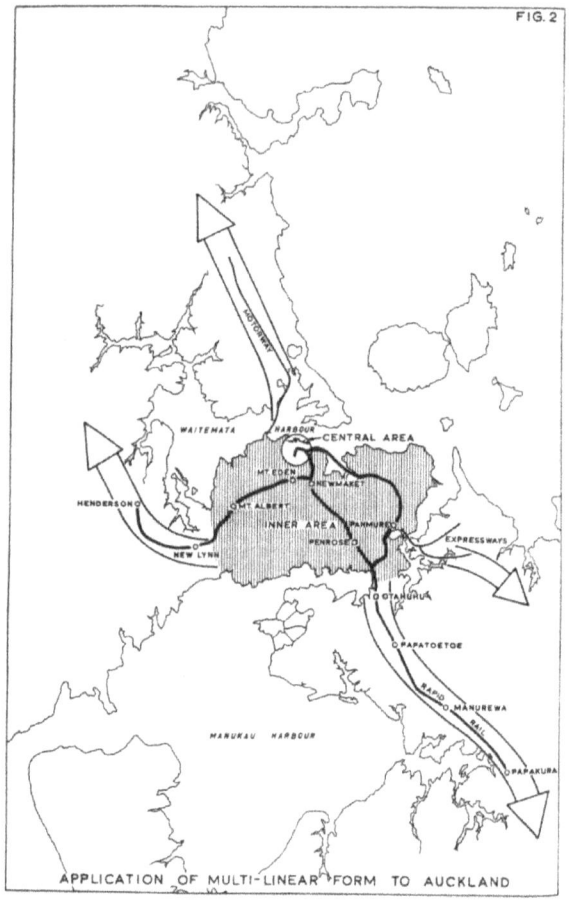

Source: Frederick W. O. Jones, Director of Planning, Auckland Regional Authority, 'Rapid rail in regional planning', in Proceedings: Auckland Rapid Rail Symposium, 15-16 August 1969, Logan Park, Auckland (Auckland Branch, New Zealand Institution of Engineers, 1969), pp. 10.-1.10, discussion 10.11-10.12.

The rapid rail proposal was known, itself, as Robbie's Rapid Rail, after its chief political champion Sir Dove-Myer Robinson, the long-serving mayor of Auckland City, which in those days covered the northern half of the central isthmus.

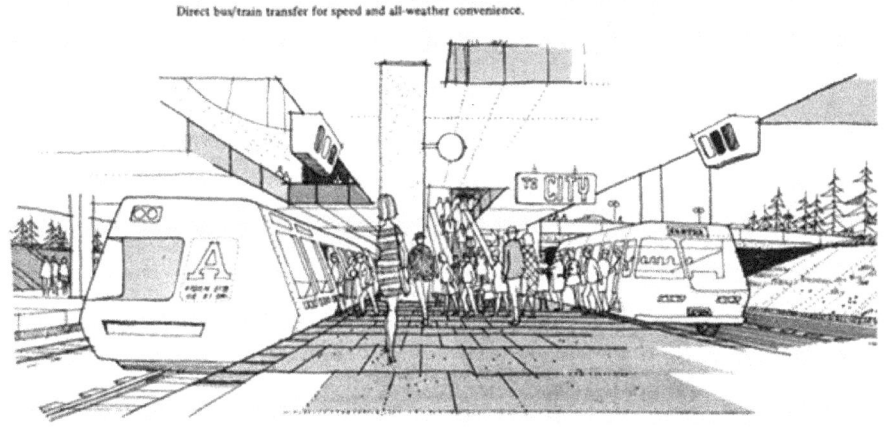

From Dove-Myer Robinson, Passenger Transport in Auckland: a report ..., Auckland Regional Authority, 1969. Crown copyright reserved.

Robinson also helped found the Auckland Regional Authority in 1963, the most significant of several attempts to unify Auckland City and its independent suburbs in a framework that would allow the built-up area, and surrounding nature-parks, to be planned and paid for as a whole.

Auckland as it might have been

RAPID TRANSIT SUBURBAN STATION

AN ALL BUS SYSTEM

From Auckland Regional Authority, Facts about the Public Passenger Transport System in Auckland, Auckland, the Authority, 1967. Crown copyright reserved.

From Pedestrians in Queen Street, *Auckland City Council Department of Planning and Social Development, 1977. Crown Copyright reserved.*

'Vulcan Lane in 1968, shortly after it was pedestrianised. A number of fashion stores can be seen — front right is La Rue Accessories, middle right Kay Marie millinery salon and front left Dion fashion store. Signage for the Druleigh College of Dressmaking can also be seen. Auckland Libraries Heritage Collections 7-A4222.' Caption by Auckland Heritage, on Facebook. Photo dated 1 July 1968, photographer unknown. Rectified and cropped from a higher resolution image supplied by Te Kura Tawhiti, Research, Heritage and Central Library, Auckland Libraries.

The parks within the built-up area, many of them long and skinny and running along the sides of streams, were also to be joined up with cycleways, so that the city would become as bikeable as Christchurch.

This idea was set out in a 1980 report to the Auckland Regional Authority, *The "Green City" concept applied to The Auckland isthmus,* re-published in a prestigious British journal called *Town Planning Review* in 1984.

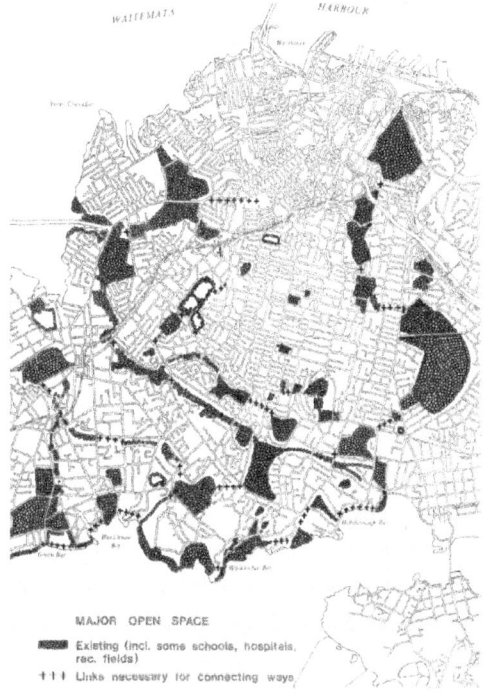

From the 'Green City' Plan for Auckland, 1980/1984. Crown Copyright reserved.

But after their announcement, each of these schemes then would be kicked for touch on the grounds that we couldn't afford it.

And that, in any case, Auckland's days of rapid growth were surely coming to an end. Many people believed that no city could possibly grow past a million in a country that depended on cows and sheep. It just didn't make sense.

And therefore, that there was no place in New Zealand for these kinds of big-city dreams, from rapid rail to pedestrianized downtown areas and networks of leafy bikeways.

On the other hand, there *was* money for road-widening and the building of motorways, if only in a reactive, a year-by-year, drip-feeding sort of a way whereby the roadworks seemed to take ages, as indeed they still do.

This was because, unlike railway schemes and associated schemes of pedestrianisation, which had to be funded upfront and largely completed in their entirety before the first train could run, the widening of roads and extension of motorways could be done bit by bit as required and financed bit by bit from petrol taxes and Diesel mileage charges earmarked for spending on the roads.

The drip feeding of funds from petrol pump and hubodometer to bulldozer also appealed to the increasing numbers of those who favoured the principle of 'user pays', even if, in truth, the market for roads was more captive than competitive.

Under this system, more cars and more trucks meant more revenue from petrol taxes and mileage charges to pay for more roads, which in turn led to more cars and trucks on the roads.

It was a virtuous circle if you were a roadbuilder, road haulier, owner of a petrol station or a panelbeater, though a vicious circle from the point of view of almost everyone else.

The Auckland Central Motorway Junction on a Sunday. Photograph by Chris Harris

Mean Streets ... Photos by Chris Harris, early 2000s

And so, because we had ceased to plan ahead in any serious way, in a city that nevertheless kept growing, the cars ate Auckland; including such former beauty spots as Grafton Gully, now largely filled with concrete.

Detail from the earlier 1949 aerial photograph of downtown Auckland, showing Grafton Gully and Grafton Bridge. Source: 'Grafton Road, Auckland', Whites Aviation Ltd: Photographs. Ref: WA-19229-F. Alexander Turnbull Library, Wellington, New Zealand. /records/22512926.

Chapter 2

'An Account of Missed Chances'

KNOWN already as Tāmaki-makau-rau, Auckland was founded as a British colonial port in 1840, the same year as the Treaty of Waitangi, receiving the status of a city in 1871.

This means that, before too long, Auckland will be two hundred years old. As Tāmaki-makau-rau, it is much older.

The new British port was cut off from its hinterland by forested, flood-prone ravines, or gullies as they were called in Auckland. These included the Grafton Gully shown in Chapter 1, Arch Hill Gully, Newton Gully, and Kingsland Gully.

In 1841, the Surveyor-General, Felton Mathew, came up with a plan for Auckland in which terraced houses would overlook the gullies.

A detail from this plan is shown on the next page.

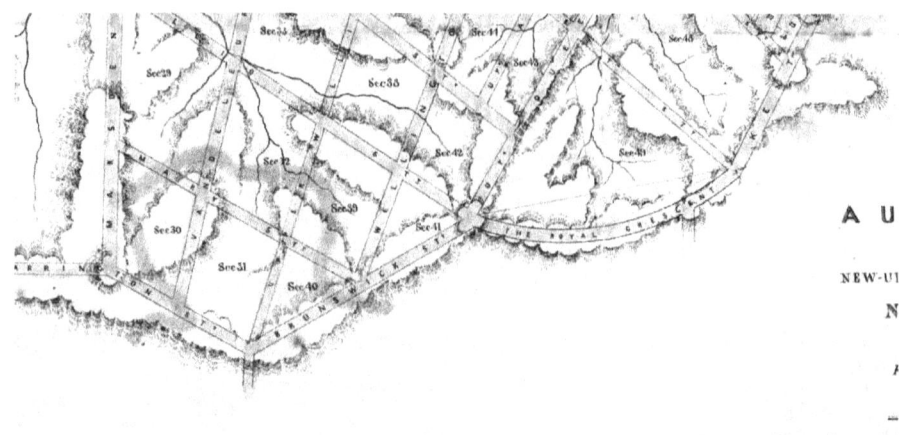

Detail of stately streets and crescents overlooking gully system from Mathew's original plan. Auckland Libraries reference NZ Map 6631, Sir George Grey Special Collections

The gullies of Auckland would be like the town belts of other settlements such as Wellington, Dunedin, and Invercargill, or for that matter the world-famous parklands of Adelaide: green lungs that would divide the most built-up area of the future city from its suburbs.

In combination with the sparkling Waitematā Harbour, the Manukau Heads, and the fifty or so green volcanoes that covered the landscape, the preserved gullies, overlooked by flats and houses, would have had the potential to make Auckland into one of the most beautiful cities in the world.

In those days Grafton Gully was regarded as one of Auckland's premier beauty spots: "a beautiful scenic reserve of native bush in the heart of the city," (*Auckland: the Gateway to New Zealand,* 1930) and "a delightful reserve of bush," within which "nothing could be more pleasant than to wander here on a summer's day–along paths cool and flecked with leafy light and shadow." (*Auckland: City of Sunshine*, 1942).

Cover of the 1930 version of Auckland: Gateway to New Zealand. *Fair dealing for the purposes of criticism and review is claimed. Library reference deleted.*

But in the 1960s and 1970s, the gullies would pass into history. Sometime in 1968, according to Hamish Keith OBE in his book *New Zealand Yesterdays,*

> An Auckland columnist, writing in the Christchurch Star, complained: "This city seems to have scant regard for the past, or for natural beauty. There have been so few letters of protest in Auckland newspapers it is reasonable to

assume that progress matters much more than the preservation of either the beautiful or the historic. Whatever stands in the way of traffic streams must go."

After some sleuthing, it turns out that this columnist was Geoffrey Webster, a former chief reporter on the *Auckland Star*. Published in the 8 June 1968 issue of the Christchurch *Star*, Webster's article was called 'Dead must give way to the living'. Its subject was that of two colonial cemeteries, one in Grafton Gully and one in the Wellington suburb of Thorndon, that were being exhumed to make room for their cities' respective motorways.

In the case of Grafton Gully, Webster contrasted an early-1900s battle to save Grafton Gully from the possible disruption of having a bridge built across it, to the indifference of a later generation to the fact that an even more disruptive motorway was now being rammed through the space that had been so carefully preserved by Auckland's forebears:

> *Oddly, there were few protests when it was announced that the Symonds Street Cemetery and Grafton Gully lay in the projected track of the complex system. . . .*
>
> *As for Grafton Gully, there would be 'a measure of disruption.' Part of its beauty would be spoilt, engineers admitted. To-day nothing is left of it. Ugliness has replaced loveliness.*

Figure 13–12: Grafton Gully on 5 February 1968, corner detail from 'Auckland Motorways, Dominion Road Interchange', Whites Aviation Ltd :Photographs. Ref: WA-67442-G. Alexander Turnbull Library, Wellington, New Zealand. http://natlib.govt.nz/records/23121284

Webster continued thus:

The beauty of Grafton Gully has gone forever. When, sixty years ago, Auckland planned to build Grafton Bridge, to link hospital and Domain area with the top of Queen Street neighbourhood, there were protests innumerable. The colonists cared. They demanded undertakings.

The graceful reinforced-concrete arch of Grafton Bridge, which spared the bush below from any need for a hefty pillar in the middle of the span—such a lengthy arch was a very new and radical idea at the time—may have been one of those undertakings.

(To look into the political origins of the design of the Grafton Bridge further would be a good topic for a student thesis.)

New Zealand's history has been called as "an account of missed chances," and in perhaps no sense have our chances been more badly missed than in the way that Auckland has turned out.

The green volcanic hills, many of them interestingly terraced by the original inhabitants of Tāmaki-makau-rau, were eventually preserved against quarrying and other forms of vandalism by a 1915 Act of Parliament.

Sadly, though, no similar act was ever passed to preserve the natural state of the gullies, to turn them into a town belt to match that of other centres.

Had that been done, Auckland would have been spared the construction of its giant downtown motorway junction, which took all four ravines and filled them with motorway concrete.

A downtown motorway junction is, basically, a terrible idea: a congestion magnet, as well as vandalistic of the city's downtown qualities.

On top of that, Auckland's frequent late-afternoon rains cut motorway capacity in half, so they either have to be double-sized, or else we accept that there will be gridlock every other afternoon peak.

Scene from This Auckland, *National Film Unit, 1967, via YouTube. Fair dealing is claimed.*

When motorways were first thought up, in the 1930s, the idea was that they would skirt around the most built-up parts of the city.

In this country, an upgraded State Highway One was originally intended to run through Puhinui, Māngere and Mount Roskill on much the same route as today's SH20 and from there around the Upper Harbour via New Lynn and Riverhead. You can read about that plan in the annual report of the Ministry of Works that appears in the *Appendix to the Journals of the House of Representatives* for 1946.

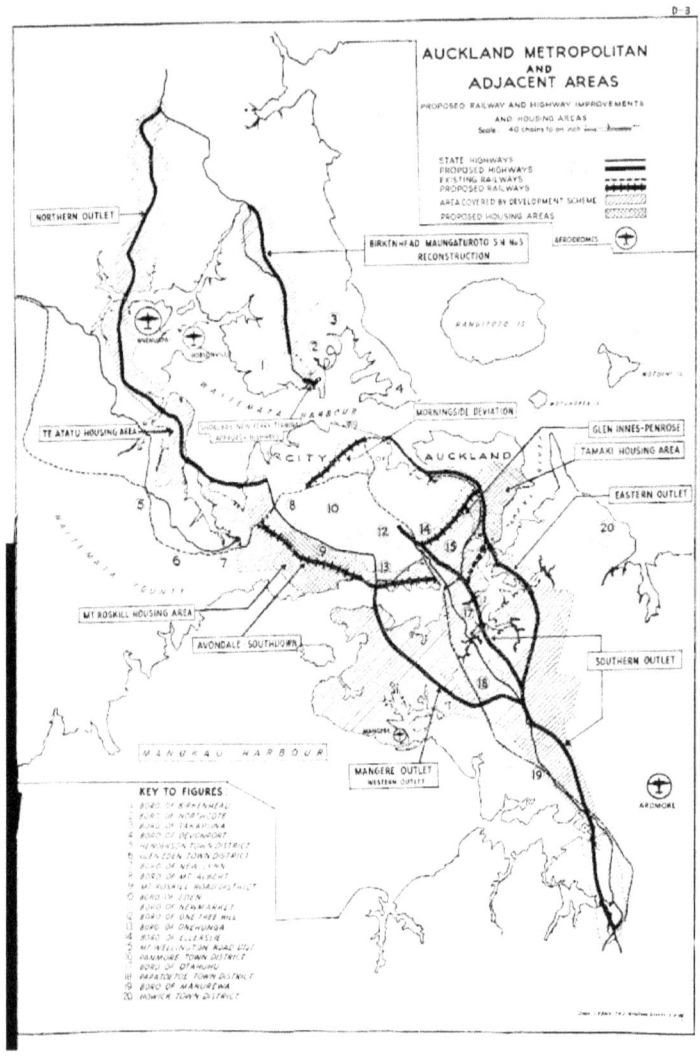

From the Appendix to the Journals of the House of Representatives, Wellington, 1946, Ministry of Works Report, via PapersPast.

And in a digest of the same plans called *The Shape of Things to Come,* also published in 1946—its title seemingly a nod to H G Wells—in which the New Zealand Government promised to electrify Auckland's railways and extend the eastern semi-circle through Ōrākei, Glen Innes and Panmure (opened in 1930) into a complete circle accessing western suburbs like Grey Lynn and Mount Roskill.

The Auckland CBD and the rising industrial area of Penrose would both be served equally by the proposed circle, at its northern and southern poles respectively. The existing Southern and Western lines would cross the circle, and a harbour bridge would extend the railway service to the North Shore. *The Shape of Things to Come* also said that special legislation had been enacted so that land could be acquired "without danger of paying an inflated price" for "great new settlements being built by the State, chiefly around Wellington, Auckland, and Christchurch."

With the main state highway skirting around the downtown area and not through it, if a person had wanted to go downtown in those days, they would have most likely caught a tram, a train, or a ferry.

Only from the mid-1950s onwards were suburban motorways brought right into the middle of the city to form a massive space-hogging junction in the part of town where space was at the greatest premium: first in the United States and eventually in Auckland.

Inner-city motorway construction was often linked to a desire to renew run-down inner-city areas that had, in the meantime, come to be populated by minorities. Minorities that the wholesale bulldozing of much of the downtown would help to evict.

The original, pre-World War II draft plan for the renewal of Auckland's downtown area had proposed the construction of more flats, in the spirit of Mathew's Plan. Most of these flats would have overlooked the harbour. The scheme would have been amazing.

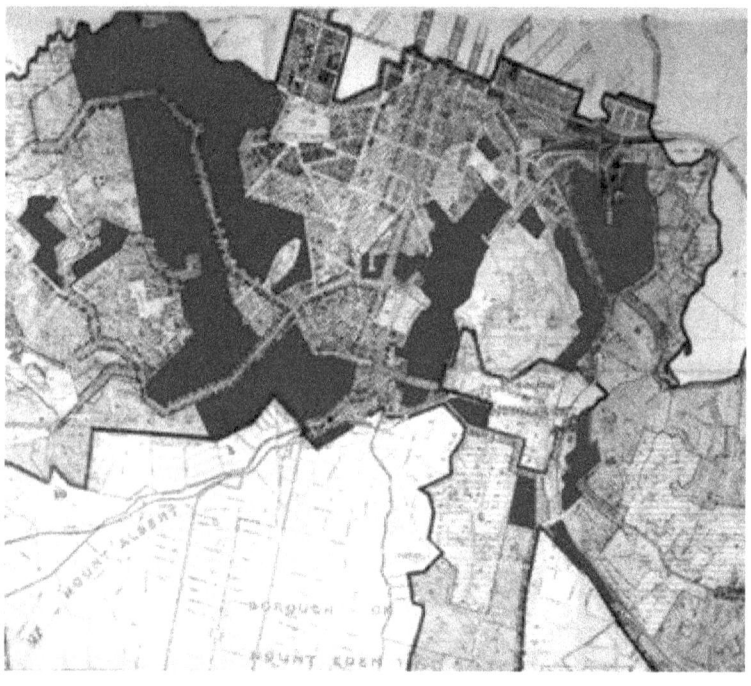

Zoning for flats (in solid colour, added for clarity) in the draft Town-Planning Scheme No. 1, Auckland City Council, 1939. Detail from Civic Survey Map of the City of Auckland Map No.1, Auckland City Council, 1930-1940. Auckland Council Archives reference: ACC 005/2240. The solid colour has been added by the present author, for clarity.

Instead, we put motorways into the ravines and depopulated the inner city, which after World War II had become the main area of Māori and Pasifika migration to the city. The demographer Wardlow Friesen has calculated, in a 2009 *New Zealand Population Review* article called 'The Demographic Transformation of Inner City Auckland,' that the innermost ten square kilometres of Auckland were depopulated by some thirty thousand between 1945 and 1990. As we saw in the Introduction, a planning map from 1968 suggests that this depopulation was not wholly unwelcome, at the time, to the powers that be.

Moreover, as the city grew larger, the suburbs where most people lived became more distant from its centre.

Increasingly cut off by waterways as they spread beyond the central isthmus, the populations of these suburbs became less interested in the fate of the downtown, or indeed, of the city as a whole.

Some fought to save His Majesty's Theatre from demolition in 1987 and to calm the traffic in the inner suburbs with tree planting, including trees in the middle of such streets as Kelmarna Avenue and Parawai Crescent.

Kelmarna Avenue. Photo by Chris Harris.

But, on the whole, there was less and less interest in what was going on outside of one's own suburb, and perhaps not much interest beyond the front gate even there.

In the days when Grafton Gully was still verdant, the City Road area on the other side of Symonds Street used to be really beautiful and picturesque as well.

From the Auckland City Libraries 'Streets' collection

In a 1964 collection of sketches called *Around Auckland*, by David More, we read of the City Road precinct that we should:

> *Leave the modern buildings of Queen Street, go down the slope of Turner Street, and you are in a pleasant area — seemingly remote though traffic hums only a few hundred yards away. Cicadas shrill among the plane trees. To the right lies steep, charming little Liverpool Street. It has a fearsome gradient but the attractive houses here cling doggedly.*

Well, that was then in the City Road area: this is now.

Photo by Chris Harris

Our failure to preserve Auckland's charms puts one in mind of a passage in a 1987 *New Zealand Journal of History* article by W. H. (Bill) Oliver, a reflection on the work of the previously mentioned Keith Sinclair, who is perhaps best known for his *History of New Zealand,* called 'A Destiny at Home'.

In that essay, Oliver wrote that Sinclair's articles and books added up to an "account of missed chances:"

This elegaic note, indeed, is often struck . . . . Maori lose; Reeves fails; Nash dwindles; Kirk dies. There is a deal more promise than fulfilment.

These are references, respectively, to the New Zealand Wars (which Sinclair was perhaps one of the first academic historians to treat as avoidable rather than inevitable), and to three of our most noted politicians, one who left the country while still young, one who only got to be Prime Minister when he was too old, and another who died at fifty-one.

However, there is some good news, of a kind that suggests Auckland's chances are not doomed to go on being missed. For, when it comes to the quality of our public transport infrastructure, cycleways, pedestrian amenity in some areas, and so on, things have improved quite a bit on where we were twenty-five years ago, at least.

Auckland is starting to turn a corner. It is just that things were so bleak in the 1990s—not to mention a certain amount of rearguard defence of 'roads and roads alone' even now—that it is, literally, taking a while.

An account of missed chances

Chapter 3
Wellington on the Waitematā: Further Reflections on Auckland as it Might Have Been

Oriental Bay, Wellington, 22 December 1959. Source: Photographic negatives and prints of the Evening Post newspaper (1865–2002), Alexander Turnbull Library, Wellington, New Zealand, EP/1959/4347-F, http://natlib.govt.nz/records/30649458. Edited to remove obtrusive overhanging eave in shot to the right in the sky area, with extraneous sky at top also cropped out.

WELLINGTON, which benefited from massive investment in electric rail in the 1930s, 1940s and 1950s, is thought by most people to be far more urbane, far more like a real city, than Auckland, even though it is much smaller.

On the face of things, it is not clear why this should be so. For both are harbour cities, with inner suburbs that slope down to the sea. Both cities also have topographically squeezed directions of further expansion, which lend themselves well to rail development.

Downtown Auckland as seen from the air, in the Auckland Summer Carnival 1923 souvenir programme. Photographer unknown.

Before the motorways, the loops of Symonds Street and Grafton Road in the east, Quay Street in the middle, and Nelson Street in the west, and in the middle the crows-foot of Queen Street and Wakefield Street, Upper Queen Street, and

Greys Avenue all seemed to give the downtown a natural coherence very much like that of downtown Wellington.

Auckland Libraries

It was a downtown seen as a worthy site for annual summer carnivals in those days, for at least a few years.

But then again, this downtown had better access to the still-natural gullies, and the vast parklands of the Auckland Domain with its new museum and winter gardens just then in the process of being built, to which access was still, as yet, unobstructed by State Highway 16.

When the motorways were first proposed, it was claimed that they would be in tunnels in most of the downtown's sensitive areas, such as at the top of Symonds Street where it becomes Upper Symonds Street, an attractive locality in those days.

Image of Upper Symonds Street from 'Expanding Auckland', Pictorial Parade №98 (1960), a composite of two frames recorded in the course of a moving camera pan from left to right, shows a park in Upper Symonds Street which was entirely excavated to create the current Symonds Street bridge over the motorway trench. Fair dealing claimed.

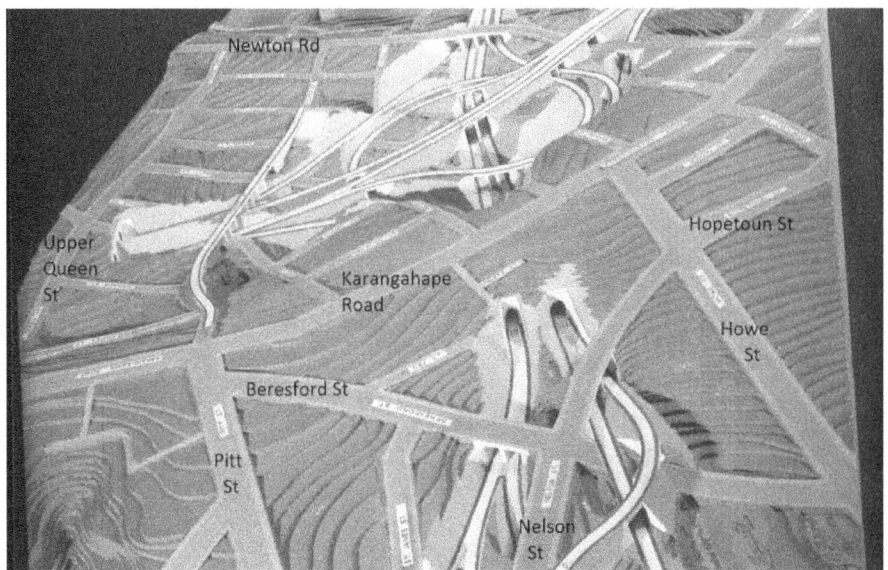

Annotated detail from photograph of 1959 Auckland motorways model, prepared by the "Town Planning Division of the Department of Works and Services," presumably of the Auckland City Council, in April 1959. The view is generally southward. To help orient the reader, some road and street names have been added by CH in black, along with the location of the former landmark Kings Arms Tavern at 59 France Street South, since replaced by a new office building, in white. France Street South was to be made continuous with Pitt Street by means of a narrow overbridge in this 1959 design, and the motorway was to run underground from Grafton Gully to Upper Queen Street. Source: Sir George Grey Special Collections, Auckland Public Libraries, image 580-3916; the model nameplate is shown in another image 580-3912.

The motorways would have been on the surface in Grafton Gully, but the Auckland Branch of the New Zealand Institute of Architects proposed a workaround in 1962, as follows:

Wellington on the Waitematā

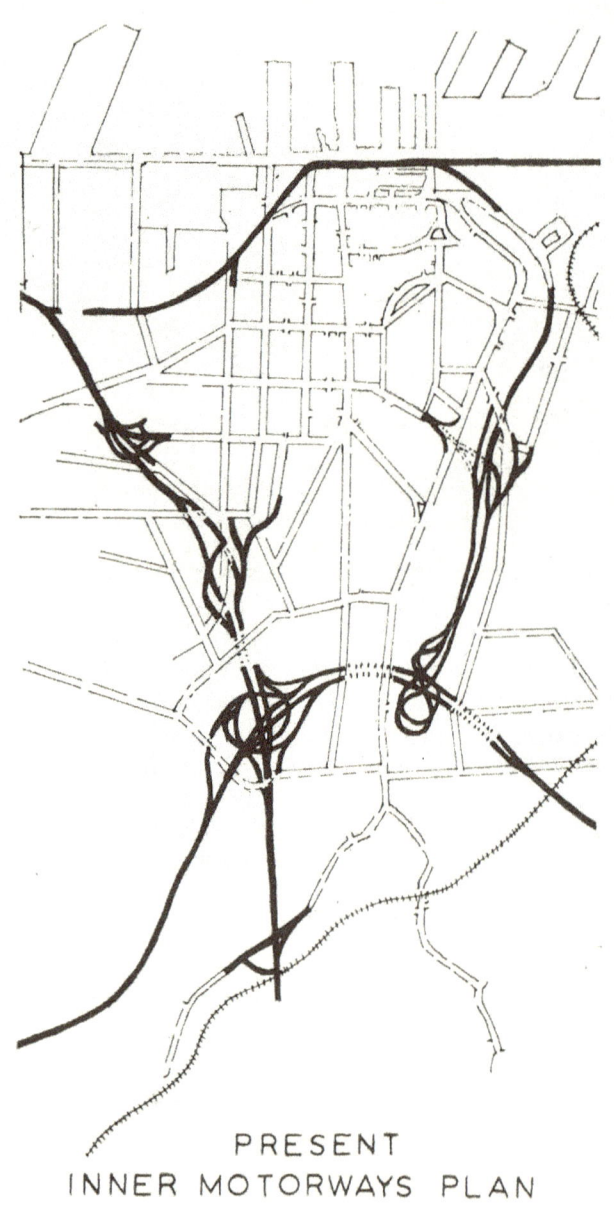

PRESENT INNER MOTORWAYS PLAN

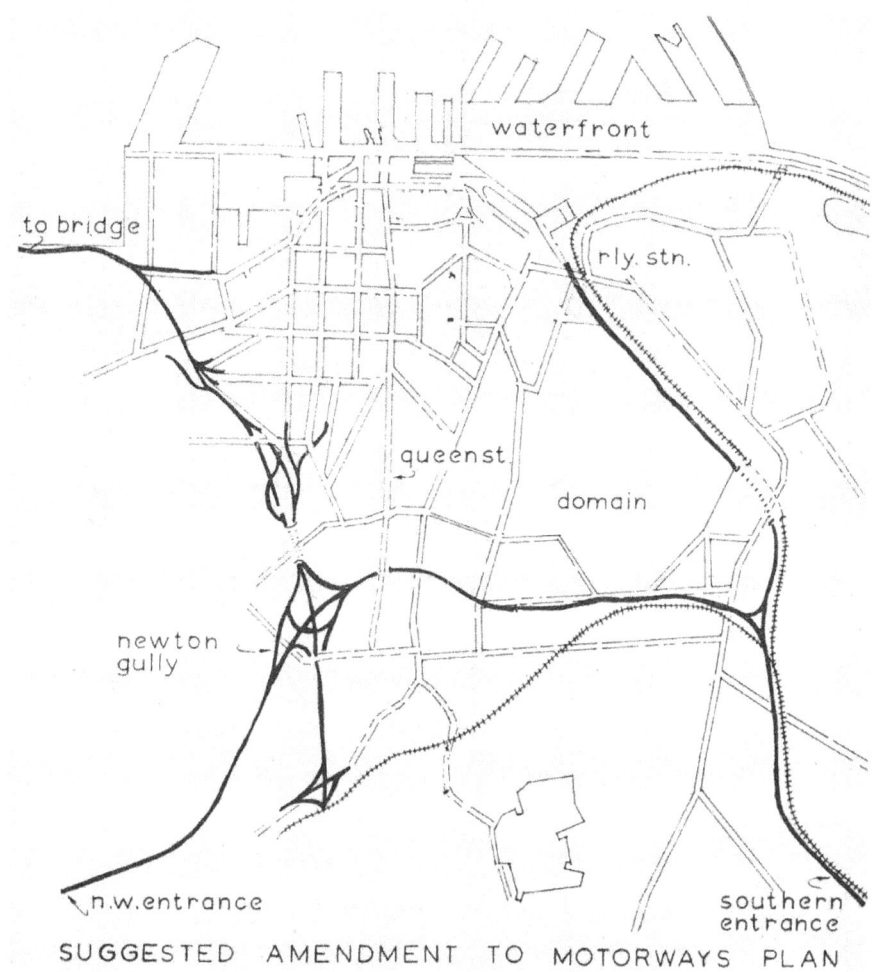

SUGGESTED AMENDMENT TO MOTORWAYS PLAN

According to the architects,

> *Catering for the motor vehicle has become the preoccupation of planners, civic authorities and engineers. The end results as they affect city and citizen have been neglected and by-passed.*

The crux of the problem then is the motor vehicle and its relation to Auckland's topography.

· · · · ·

Having provided for bringing people into the city by fast transit methods, a closer look at the efficiency of the inner-city motorway system is possible. The point is that geographically Auckland denies the need for such a scheme.

The whole plan is a misconception and must be amended to allow the city to flourish. Let the main motorway enter Auckland via Green Lane and Newmarket through Newton Gully to the north-western outlet as a regional link and then simply bring feeder routes into the three terminal areas as discussed.

This direct approach would simplify the layout of the whole inner city road system and literally break the encircling ring that perturbs many people. In effect —

(a) The Grafton Gully complex would be eliminated

(b) The elevated waterfront link would be eliminated

(c) The Newton Gully interchange would be simplified

. . . . .

Grafton Gully would be preserved in its natural state and millions of pounds saved. The feeder route would be well clear of the university development and desirable high density housing areas which look into Grafton Gully.

(The source for these graphics and text is referenced at the end of the chapter.)

In the same year, 1962, the Ministry of Works engineer in charge of building the motorways retired and accused the authorities of a "motor car complex." There was actually quite a lot of knowledgeable opposition to way things were going in Auckland but, for whatever reason, it never built up enough of a head of popular steam to force a turnaround.

A copy of the following article was donated to Chris Harris by a member of the public, some twenty years ago: it is not in the microfilm record (which occasionally misses a page), though it does exist in a paper original at the National Library in Wellington.

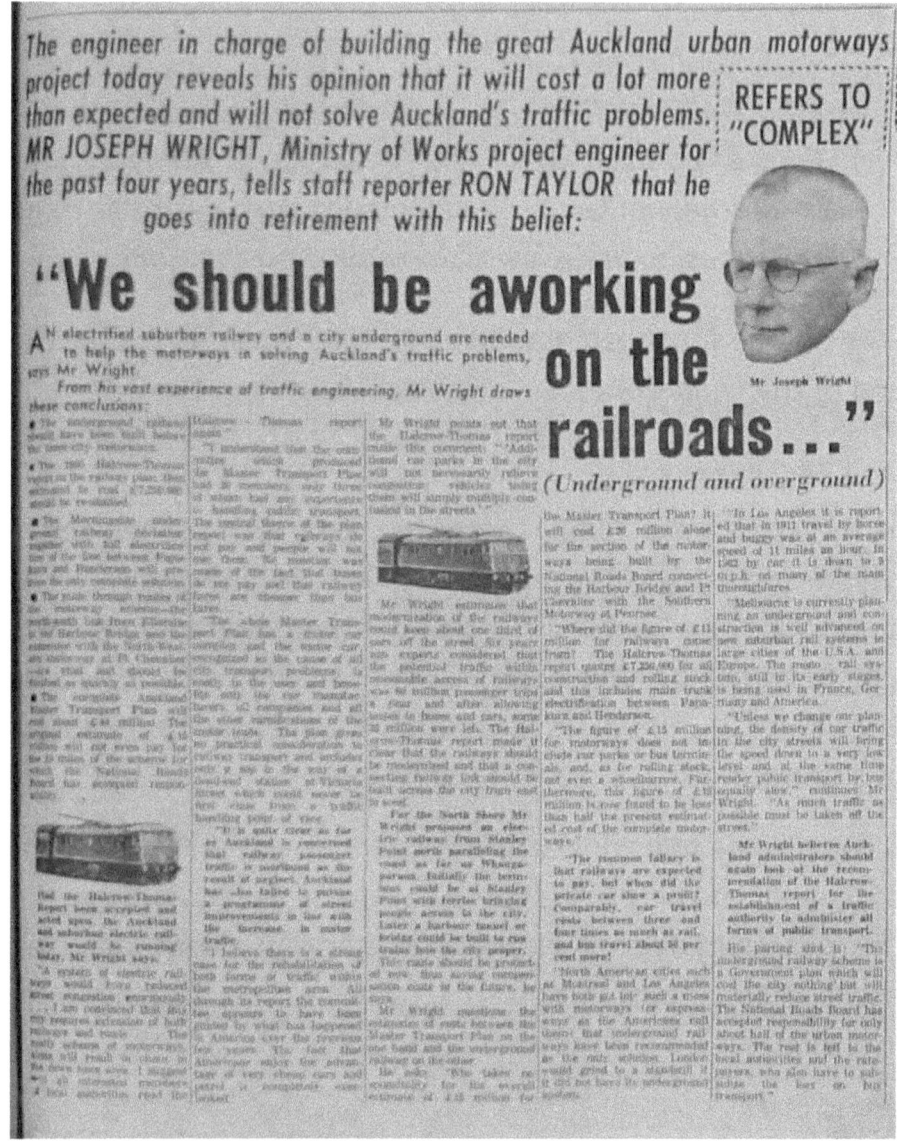

Auckland Star, 7 July 1962. © Stuff.co.nz

That Auckland could have turned out differently is made clear by the fate of the Canadian city of Vancouver, in a very similar geographical setting, in which the Burrard inlet and its three narrows double for the Waitemata and the mudflats of the Fraser River Delta for the Manukau Harbour.

Arriving in Vancouver on a misty humid evening," wrote a Kiwi visitor named Peter Blish in an account published in the *Weekly News* of 29 April 1953 (p. 22) "I thought it could have doubled for Auckland even down to its North Shore, which is always lit up at night."

Yet Vancouver, famously, has no downtown motorway junction. The nearest the motorway gets to the city centre is six kilometres to the east of Canada Place, the local equivalent of Auckland's Aotea Square.

As mentioned earlier, in this country, State Highway One was to run through Mount Roskill and around the Upper Harbour. We see that scheme, for instance, in the *Appendix to the Journals of the House of Representatives* for 1946, in the Ministry of Works section, which is now online.

The connections between downtown Auckland and the North Shore were to be purely local: which is probably why the Auckland Harbour Bridge was built with only four lanes to begin with. If you wanted to go downtown, you would have caught a tram, a train, or a ferry.

Which is pretty much how it still is in Vancouver except that many riders use its famous driverless Skytrain.

Actually, there was a scheme for an Auckland-style 'Spaghetti Junction' in Vancouver, complete with motorways in open trenches with bridges on top, the kind that was eventually built after the public had been won over with promises of tunnels.

This was rejected and was mocked … A story by John Mackie called 'What Might Have Been', published in the *Vancouver Sun* in January 2008, describes the scheme for a downtown freeway junction in Vancouver as a wacky might-have-been:

> *The* Vancouver Sun's *files are brimming with stories about politicians and planners who wanted to build all sorts of freeways and transit systems, but failed. Some of the plans look interesting, others are simply nuts. . . .*
>
> *The most mind-boggling plans were for the freeway systems in the late 1950s and 1960s. If they had been built, Vancouver would have been a very, very different place.*
>
> *The wackiest proposal was to build a giant trench through downtown. . . .*
>
> *A 1960 drawing of the big ditch at Comox and Thurlow shows a dizzying complex of roads and cloverleafs. Try to imagine the Trans-Canada Highway in Burnaby plopped down in the middle of the West End, only bigger (it was eight lanes wide, and 10 metres deep).*

It's hard to imagine what the ditch designers were thinking. They planned bridges — bridges! — on Nelson, Barclay, Haro, Robson, Georgia and Hastings streets....

Looking back from 2007, the big ditch looks completely ludicrous...

Well, if so, it looks like the joke was on Auckland, as we can see from several images on the pages that follow.

Looking westward over Newton, Auckland, 23 July 1986. Source: Newton, Auckland. Whites Aviation Ltd :Photographs. Ref: WA-78871-F. Alexander Turnbull Library, Wellington, New Zealand. http://natlib.govt.nz/records/22316121

Newton off-ramp from Northwestern Motorway, Auckland, 3 December 1986. Source: Newton, Auckland. Whites Aviation Ltd :Photographs. Ref: WA-79209-F. Alexander Turnbull Library, Wellington, New Zealand. http://natlib.govt.nz/records/23129613

Detail from Extension of motorway under Grafton Bridge, Auckland. Whites Aviation Ltd (3 December 1986): Photographs. Ref: WA-79197-F. Alexander Turnbull Library, Wellington, New Zealand. http://natlib.govt.nz/records/22325123

Auckland's Grafton Gully with contemporary motorway, looking southward. Imagery ©2018 Google, DigitalGlobe, CNES/Airbus, Data SIO, NOAA, US Navy, NGA, GEBCO, Landsat/Copernicus. Map Data ©2018 Google, MapData Sciences Pty Ltd, PSMA.

The Symonds Street Overbridge. Photo by Chris Harris

The as-built Symonds Street Overbridge over the motorway trench. The building with the Ford sign in the 1960 newsreel appears blue in this modern Google image from a similar but more elevated viewpoint, looking southward. Imagery ©2018 Google, DigitalGlobe, Landsat/Copernicus, Data/SIO, NOAA, US Navy, NGA, GEBCO, CNES/Airbus, Map Data ©2018 Google, Map DataSciences Pty Ltd, PSMA.

A plaque on the Symonds Street Overbridge, where the park at the top of Symonds Street used to be, proudly announces the presence of "100 major structures" on the Auckland motorway system as of 1990, the date of New Zealand's widely commemorated Treaty of Waitangi sesquicentennial.

Photo by Chris Harris

Online, Engineering New Zealand's heritage page on the Auckland Motorways states, as of the time of writing, that "Auckland's comprehensive motorway network had its genesis in the 1950s. At almost 90 kilometres long, the system contains more than 90 bridges, including the Auckland Harbour Bridge."

According to recent news articles, downtown Auckland's Karangahape Road, has (for some reason) been voted one of the coolest and most interesting streets on the planet.

Well, all we can say is, imagine how cool Karangahape Road would have been if its buildings had not been bisected by the motorway, over which this famous road passes in the form of — you guessed it — a bridge.

Note: the architectural critique of the Grafton Gully motorway comes from Stephan A. Jelacich ('Registered Architect'), 'New ideas on inner-city roading needs: architects put forward their proposals', diagrams and text in Fred C. Symes, ed, *Auckland Expanding to Greatness,* Breckell & Nicholls, Auckland, 1962, pp 210–212, text at 210, 211–212, sketches reproduced with the permission of the New Zealand Institute of Architects.

Chapter 4

Countryfied

WRITING in 1921, an anonymous columnist named Dionysus contended, in an article called 'New Zealand Nationality / Does it Exist Yet?' that:

> *Pre-eminence in Rugby football and dairy products is not enough. I want to see our scientists, our artists, our writers (when discovered), encouraged so that they might put New Zealand's name on the map as a country which produces ideas as well as butter-fat, as a nation that has spirit as well as population and area.*

The alarming thing is that that passage could have been published in last week's *New Zealand Listener*. For much of our history we have tended to think of New Zealand as an essentially rural country, its prosperity guaranteed mainly by muscular pursuits rather than dexterous ones.

Even though only one New Zealander in ten now lives and works in rural districts, the cities are treated as somehow not a part of the 'real' New Zealand.

This attitude extends to the degree of focus with which we think about the largest city in the country, Auckland.

In all its years of existence since 1966, Auckland University Press has not published one book primarily concerned with contemporary Auckland Issues.

Even the book *Being Māori in the City: Indigenous Everyday Life in Auckland* turns out to have been by a visiting Canadian anthropologist, Natacha Gagné, whose research was paid for in Canada. And to top it all off, *Being Māori in the City* was not published locally but by the University of Toronto Press.

This is surely half the problem. It is time to start taking our urban condition seriously!

This countrymindedness not only held back the study of Auckland, but even extended to the way we saw Auckland itself.

John F. Kennedy once declared, in a speech to Yale University students and faculty in 1962, that:

> ... *the great enemy of truth is very often not the lie-- deliberate, contrived and dishonest--but the myth-- persistent, persuasive, and unrealistic. Too often we hold fast to the cliches of our forebears. We subject all facts to a prefabricated set of interpretations. We enjoy the comfort of opinion without the discomfort of thought.*

And there is a very good example of what Kennedy meant, right here in Auckland. For, throughout the second half of the twentieth century, transport and planning in Auckland was overshadowed by a myth to the effect that Auckland was one of the most sprawling cities in the world: too sprawling for public transport to be effective.

In the Auckland *State Highway Strategy* for the year 2000, Transit New Zealand, now Waka Kotahi/NZTA, wrote that:

> *The overall residential population density of the Auckland urban area is under 300 people per square kilometre of land area. This is very low compared to large overseas cities which can typically have population densities of well over 1,000 residents per square kilometre... [The] growth strategy, which is expected to result in some increase in residential population densities, particularly within proposed "liveable communities," will be supported by improved public passenger transport. Nevertheless, for the foreseeable future Auckland's land use patterns will continue to rely primarily on private road-based transport to provide a safe and efficient transport system. Furthermore, the topography of the region means that this road-based transport system will continue to be focused on a few major transport corridors, including the existing motorway corridors....*

This was a fantastic figure that suggested a city fifty kilometres by sixty kilometres in extent for a population, then, of a million or so. Was it a typo?

Yet the long-serving Auckland University Geography Department Head Professor Kenneth B. Cumberland, who should have known better, made a similar claim in an essay called 'The Essential Nature of Auckland,' published in the book *Auckland at Full Stretch* in 1977:

> *For its population, Auckland spreads further than any other city: it has very low densities of population. On estimates of the current population, Auckland has no more than 7.7 persons per ha (3.1 per acre). This is only 770 per square kilometre (or 2,000 per square mile). It is less than in many rural and purely agricultural communities in other lands. Such dispersion renders the centre difficult and expensive to reach, and makes the downtown area a human desert at the weekend. It makes the provision of public transport expensive; it makes even a rapid rail system difficult to justify, and the journey to work time-consuming and expensive.*

In reality, the density of the built-up areas of Auckland is much higher; such low densities are arrived at by dividing the total population into the overall political or census area of Auckland, which is of course strictly meaningless from a planning point of view unless one is championing eventual sprawl into the whole of that area, as if it would be a good thing. And not all of that area is buildable in any case.

Even those critical of cars, motorways, and traffic tended to get neutralized by the density myth. A consultancy working for the Auckland Regional Council in 2000 and 2001, Hill Young Cooper, found that 330,000 people dwelt, at that time, in census mesh block units extending one to two kilometres from the existing Auckland railway tracks within a built-up area that had a total population of 866,000: basically, Auckland south of the North Shore.

Prime Minister Helen Clark—a veteran Auckland Labour MP—is recorded as having responded to the Hill Young Cooper analysis with disbelief, exclaiming in 2001, as reported in a 2002 *New Zaland Herald* story called 'Those bludgers north of the Bombays . . .', and elsewhere, that "most Aucklanders don"t live within cooee of a train station."

Which was technically true. But 330,000 out of 866,000 south of the Waitematā were in a position to bike to the train station withing five minutes or so. Moreover, the train tracks also ran through many employment areas, as industrial and commercial zones were focused on the railways in the old days, and have remained much the same (save for the North Shore, of course)

The art critic Hamish Keith, no fan of the automobile either, nonetheless wrote in a 4 July 2004 *Sunday Star-Times* article called 'Stop rubbishing the CBD', that:

The greatest puzzle in this part of the world is just how reluctant Auckland has always been to come to terms with its actual size. The Auckland region sprawls over an area big enough to hold greater London twice and still have room for Paris and Manhattan. Shanghai holds a population 10 times that of Auckland in an area not much bigger than Manukau City [in South Auckland]. It is little wonder then that 50 years ago the short-sighted city fathers seized on the car as Auckland's salvation and dumped all the more sensible options in its favour.

Again, this is all quite misleading unless one is speaking of political boundaries. Moreover, as we have seen in the map from 1949 above, Auckland was still quite compact in those days. It is true that the more or less contiguously built-up parts of Auckland now extend some 60 km from north to south. But they do so on a linear and coastal alignment between two harbours that, if anything, increases the case for rail and does not mean that the city is too sprawling for public transport to work.

The myth of an Auckland too sprawling for public transport to work occasionally met with mild criticism but was never seriously taken on by local scholars. It was eventually busted at the turn of the millennium by a couple of people based at Australian universities, an Australian urbanist named Paul Mees and a New Zealand émigré now based at the Royal Melbourn Institute of Technology, Jago Dodson.

Even so, as late as 2006, its legacy of fatalism endured. How else to explain Helen Clark's finance minister Michael Cullen's resistance, in that year, to calls for Auckland commuter rail electrification, telling Aucklanders that they should make do with the bus and road-widening because "buses need roads too?" This peevish remark is recorded in Part 2 of Michael Tritt's 2006 documentary 'Auckland, City of Cars', available on YouTube, a documentary that also deals directly with the great Auckland density myth and features an interview with Paul Mees, who is sadly no longer with us.

Things have since improved. But for at least forty-five years, given that it was already present in the text of the strongly pro-motorway *Master Transportation Plan for Metropolitan Auckland*, published in a glossy form in 1956, the myth of an Auckland too sprawling for urban public transport to be effective tended to paralyse even those who were opposed to Auckland's transformation into a city of cars. It serves as a very good example of what happens when a city does not have academics who are serious about pushing back against myth. That the Australian cavalry had to come in and save us is a real disgrace.

Notes:

The quote from 'Dionysus' is also reproduced in Keith Sinclair's last scholarly book *A Destiny Apart: New Zealand's Search for National Identity* (1986), at p. 48.

The most canonical example of Mees and Dodson's debunking of the great Auckland density myth is their paper 'The American Heresy: Half a century of transport planning in Auckland,' given as a presentation to the joint conference of New Zealand Geographical Society and the Australian Institute of Geographers at the University of Otago, Dunedin, in 2002. A draft dating back to 1999 can be found online.

Chapter 5

Our Forgotten Land Banks

MUCH has been made, lately, of the social housing achievements of European cities like Vienna, with their huge municipal land banks. The success of those sorts of cities in overcoming homelessness and housing scarcity puts many English-speaking cities to shame.

Forty years on from the coming of Rogernomics, we have forgotten that, until the 1980s, we had a similar policy in New Zealand to that of the Viennese.

In the early 1980s, public authorities maintained huge suburban land banks in New Zealand. One such example was the New Zealand Housing Corporation land bank that covered 687 hectares — nearly seven square kilometres — in the part of Auckland's North Shore that is known as Albany.

On the next page, you can see an old newspaper clipping of a proposal to develop this land, held in a Ministry of Works and Development file in the possession of Archives New Zealand.

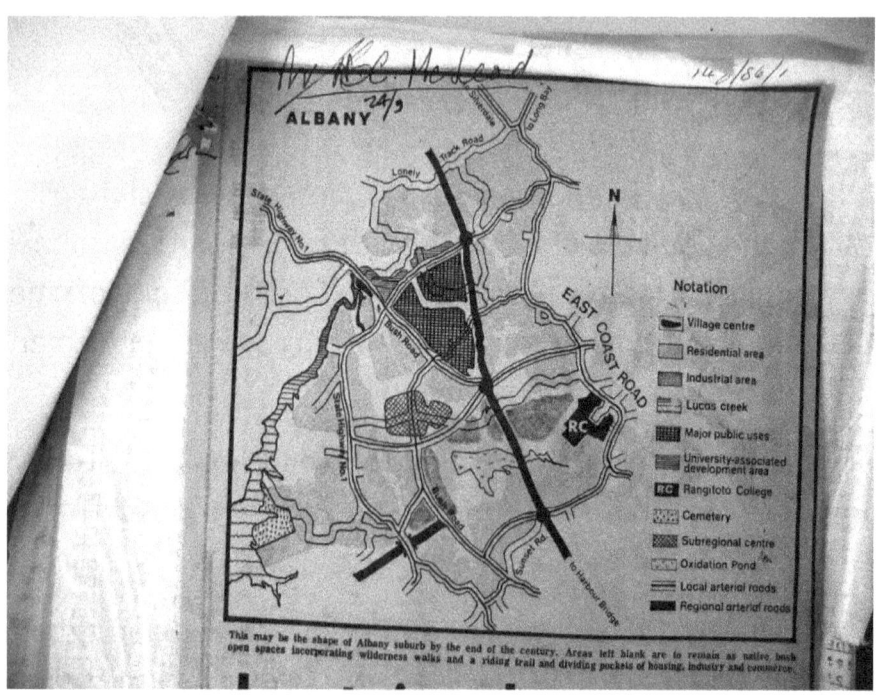

A Ministry of Works and Development plan for the public development of Albany which appeared in the Auckland Star on 14 August 1974, in the former Ministry of Works and Development file 149/86/1, held by Archives New Zealand in Wellington. The Auckland Star content, mostly sourced from the MWD in any case, is reproduced as fair dealing.

On the following page, there is another such proposal.

An alternative scheme for the same area, in the same file. The dotted areas outlined in brown are proposed residential; the purple hatching industrial; the red full hatching town centres; the areas outlined in yellow for named facilities. The area shown as university and hospital correspond to the present-day Albany Centre between the Albany Expressway, State Highway One and Oteha Valley Road: the university was relocated, and the hospital never eventuated. The Albany Scenic Reserve survives today as a vestige of what was a much more ambitious green belt scheme in 1974. Crown Copyright Reserved.

These land banks were developed, in the public domain, by such agencies as the Housing Corporation, the Ministry of

Works and Development, and even some of the larger municipalities, such as the Manukau City Council which, at the other end of Auckland, was in charge of developing its own city centre.

Manukau City Centre shopping mall, Auckland. Whites Aviation Ltd: Photographs. Ref: WA-73691-G. Alexander Turnbull Library, Wellington, New Zealand /records/22741546.

According to New Zealand's 1975 *Official Yearbook*,

> *Such has been the demand for State development in Auckland and Wellington that it has been necessary to acquire large areas of land in these metropolitan areas, which, when developed over a number of years, has*

resulted in the creation of new towns. These have been comprehensively planned, and developed sites have been made available for central commercial, industrial and administrative areas as well as civic and neighbourhood amenities. At present the three existing instances of development at this scale are Porirua City, near Wellington, and Otara and Mangere townships within Manukau City, south of Auckland.

In accordance with continuing Government policy, the planning of these towns and State development generally has recognised the need to conserve land and gain as much return from the installation of municipal services as possible. For these reasons, particular attention has been paid to subdivisional pattern and, where appropriate, medium-density housing to an acceptable level has been introduced. In addition, a measure of building of medium and high-density residential accommodation has been undertaken in inner city areas in Auckland and Wellington.

Further substantial areas of land have been acquired in the Albany Basin in Auckland for future development. A planning exercise, aimed at achieving the integration of State with private housing in the Albany area and the creation of a high standard of urban environment is currently being undertaken by local authority and departmental officers. Commencement of land development is timed for late 1974 or 1975. A large-scale development is also planned for Rolleston, south of Christchurch. (p. 517)

The state's possession of these land banks dated in one way or another all the way back to colonial times

In 1881, Sir Julius Vogel, formerly the Treasurer and Premier of the Colony of New Zealand, published an open letter in which he went so far as to colourfully declare that any of his successors who sold off the public land bank should "be hung":

Meanwhile the railway estate will develop, and in the course of time become enormously valuable. . . . Look at the value of [private enterprise] railway systems where fighting and competition go on in every direction over almost every mile, and then ask what must be the value of a [state] system in which the costly warfare will of necessity be absent. Twenty years hence the railways of New Zealand will be enormously valuable. . . . The Government which divested the colony of its contingent profits derivable from keeping the railways for the benefit of the State would, in my opinion, deserve to be hung. Scarcely less should be the punishment of a State which sacrificed the public lands which those railways make every year more valuable . . .

This letter can be found online as 'Sir Julius Vogel and the New Zealand Railways', text of a letter of 21 April 1881, posted from London to Mr Oswald Curtis of Nelson and reproduced in *The Press,* Christchurch, 15 June 1881.

One of the reasons for retention of large public land banks for future development was that comprehensive mobility planning, of the sort that would make it easy to get around by alternatives to the automobile, required a similarly comprehensive planning system.

According to the 1946 government film *Housing in New Zealand,* accessible on YouTube,

> *Self-contained communities are being built on the outskirts of our cities. This project ... is planned so that the houses will surround a park in which will be sports grounds and schools and shops and theatres. Paths will link them all together — where the path meets the road there will be an overbridge. When the children go to school or we go shopping we won't be dodging cars and in our shopping areas we will find a series of courts free of traffic, planned to group shops and offices and recreation.*

Another reason was that public land banks were also held to be the only way to guarantee the future affordability of housing, and prevent undue speculation and windfalls, in the often-cramped geographical setting of New Zealand's cities.

In a 1977 publication called *Auckland: The Costs of Growth,* a joint working group from the Ministry of Works and

Development and the Auckland Regional Authority therefore contended that:

> The group sees a need for a greater degree of public ownership and development of land if development strategies are to be more carefully directed and the social provisions for community life met more easily. (pp. 20–21)

And that:

> Land should be viewed as a non-renewable community-owned resource and not be treated as a profit-generating commodity. (p. 153)

During the Rogernomic era and on into the 1990s the land banks would be privatised, quite often as it seems for small fractions of what the land would eventually be worth in a market where the state was no longer continually suppressing the price of housing.

As, for instance, in a case documented by Chris Harris in a story called 'Ticky Tacky Death of a Dream' (*Metro,* June 2011), in which the government sold off 127 hectares of development land in its Albany estate for $21 million in 1994; a sum which even then was not much for so big a chunk of Albany.

Ironically, an 8 March 2024 front-page article in the Wellington newspaper *The Post,* 'One family to build them all', notes that just one family, the Callenders, now owns nearly all the land zoned for the City of Wellington's future expansion. This takes the form of a land bank of 542 hectares, nearly as big as the old Housing Corporation land bank in Albany.

In the meantime, the price of housing has exploded, in the manner documented in a remarkable recent graph by the economists Shamubeel and Selena Eaqub:

The growth of housing unaffordability in New Zealand. Graph supplied by Shamubeel Eaqub; used with permission

This graph actually understates the decline in New Zealand housing affordability since the 1960s, since, toward the left-hand side, household income would normally have been that of a single male worker with a stay-at-home wife, while toward the right-hand side, both partners would be working flat out to pay the mortgage. Relative to incomes, the price of the deposit today is about what the entire house and section cost in the days of Keith Holyoake.

The privatisation of the land banks was not the only reason for the collapse of housing affordability in New Zealand, but it was a major contributing factor.

Note

As regards the Albany estate as it was in the 1970s, it is to be found in Ministry of Works and Development Plan for Albany, 'Modified Steering Committee' option. Source: Albany Basin Development [Archives Reference AADX W3149 44 149/86/11], Archives New Zealand / The Department of Internal Affairs Te Tari Taiwhenua. The scheme publicised in the *Auckland Star* on 14 August 1974 appears above a covering article 'Lost in the storm — hope for the future' by John Roughhan [sic]. At the time, the Labour Government intended that the 687- hectare public land bank be made even larger: see Plan HDA (329) M 162/R2 'Plan of proposed land to be acquired for sub-regional centre and industrial purposes' in the same MWD file series.

On *Housing in New Zealand,* there is a colour film of the same title focused on the nuts and bolts of building. The one we have referenced is a black and white documentary focused on social issues.

Chapter 6

Getting Back on Track

IT'S hard, now, to recall how run-down Auckland's railway network was in the 1990s and at the turn of the millennium. Here are some photos of the Kingsland Railway Station, close to Eden Park, around the year 2003.

Photos of the old Kingsland Railway Station, by Chris Harris

It's a lot different today, of course. The old station was demolished in 2003, shortly after the photos above were taken, and a new station was built in 2004, with further upgrades in time for the 2011 Rugby World Cup.

Photos of the upgraded Kingsland Railway Station, by Chris Harris

Passenger rail services were nearly terminated altogether in the mid-1980s, but they held on, just. A major breakthrough came in 1993, when 1930s-era rolling stock on its last legs was replaced by Perth's superannuated diesel trains, still new and fresh by New Zealand standards (Perth was electrifying its system at that time).

And then in 2003, with the opening of the new Britomart rail station at the foot of Queen Street, thanks to the efforts of Christine Fletcher. Remember, this was when Kingsland still looked as it did in the first set of photos just above.

Electric commuter train arriving at the newly electrified Britomart underground station, 27 April 2014. Photo by 'Sitedmambo', CC BY-SA 3.0 via Wikimedia Commons. The train is given as an AMP class Electrical Multiple Unit in the original caption.

But there was much more to be done.

As far back as the early-to-mid 1990s, when Mary Jane Walker was on the Auckland City Council and Chris Harris was Chair of the Mount Albert Community Board, some of us in local government were advocating a rapid public transport route to the airport. There was a bus, but it went round the houses in places like Mount Eden and got down to the airport in its own good time, congestion permitting.

The 1990s was the real nadir of Auckland public transport fortunes, at least before the shiny "new" Perth trains went in (new by Auckland standards: some dated back to 1968).

Mary Jane was on the Council representing the Alliance but also the Campaign for Public Transport, which we'd helped to found.

There had been very few of us in the CPT back then, and unfortunately the majority of councillors and officials involved in transport planning in Auckland were also pretty skeptical about our entreaties. For the reasons given above, they thought that Auckland was too sprawling to warrant expenditure on a high-quality public transport system, at least for the foreseeable future.

As late as 1999, the Auckland *Regional Land Transport Strategy* (RLTS) had high quality public transport to the airport as something to be looked into at some time in the future, which in those days was really code for 'never'.

This was what we were going to have to make do with by 2021.

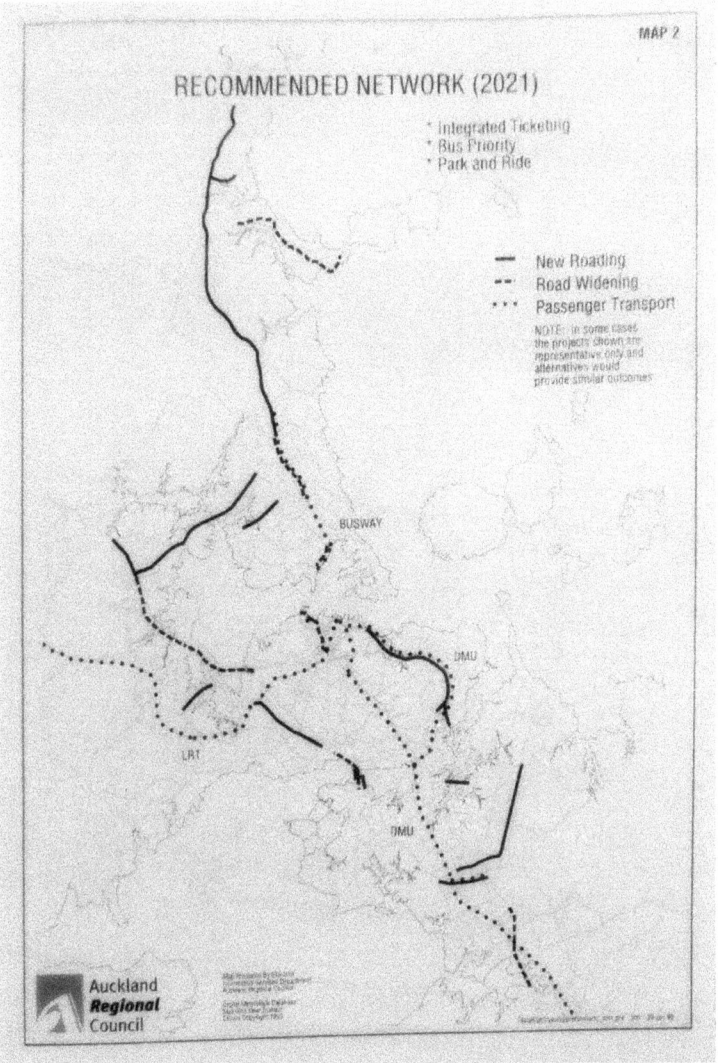

From Transport and Land Use in the Auckland Region, *by the Auckland Regional Growth Forum (January 1999)*

And even as Auckland hit a projected two million:

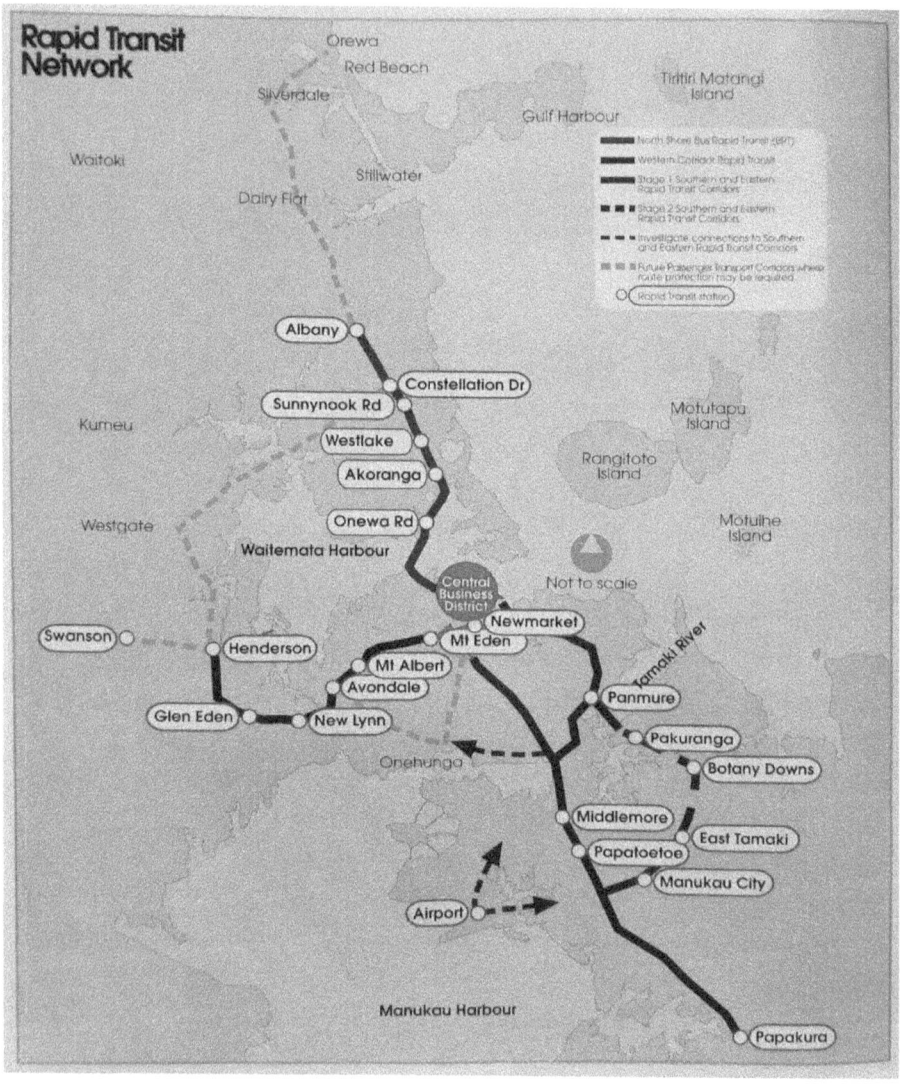

From Managing the Region's Transport System, *an official summary of the 1999 Auckland RLTS*

We've made a surprising amount of progress since those days, with Britomart, the City Rail Link tunnels and stations being dug at long last: which, after rail electrification itself, was always the single biggest and most revolutionary component of the old Robbie's Rapid Rail scheme.

The tunnels enable the trains to go through the central city in a loop, not round and round of course but rather coming in from an outer suburb and then efficiently back out again without having to reverse back out to Newmarket, as they have done up to now, while at the same time taking advantage of several new stations around the loop. Whence the bold logo of the Auckland Rapid Transit Directorate, from 1974 (love those seventies graphics!)

Logo adopted by the Auckland Rapid Transit Directorate, 1974. Source: Auckland Rapid Transit Directorate, Auckland Rapid Transit: Report to Government, 1974, held in the Level 2 Reading Room of the Auckland Public Library. Crown Copyright Reserved.

The formation of a Directorate reporting to central Government, to develop things to that point, was the high-water mark of Robbie's Rapid Rail.

Sadly, the waters then receded. All the same, fifty years late is still better than never! Even if, in fact, it now looks more like it is going to be a little more than fifty years, with earlier predictions of opening in 2024 proving optimistic.

Image via the gallery at City Rail Link

Plus, we have seen the development of the Northern Busway, better train station and ferry terminals, more and better bus shelters, real-time passenger information, integrated ticketing via what is now the AT Hop Card and, of course, the electrification of the Auckland passenger railways.

One idea that slowly came to be accepted, as well, was that of an integrated passenger network with frequent services and transfers, an idea championed by Paul Mees in his books *A Very Public Solution* (2000) and *Transport for Suburbia* (2009).

In 2013, the public transport advocacy group Greater Auckland, successor to our tiny Campaign for Public Transport, proposed a 'Congestion-Free Network' (CFN) that included a busway to the airport from the east, interchanging at Puhinui.

A few years on, in May 2017, the CFN was updated to include light rail from the city to the airport as well.

Getting back on track

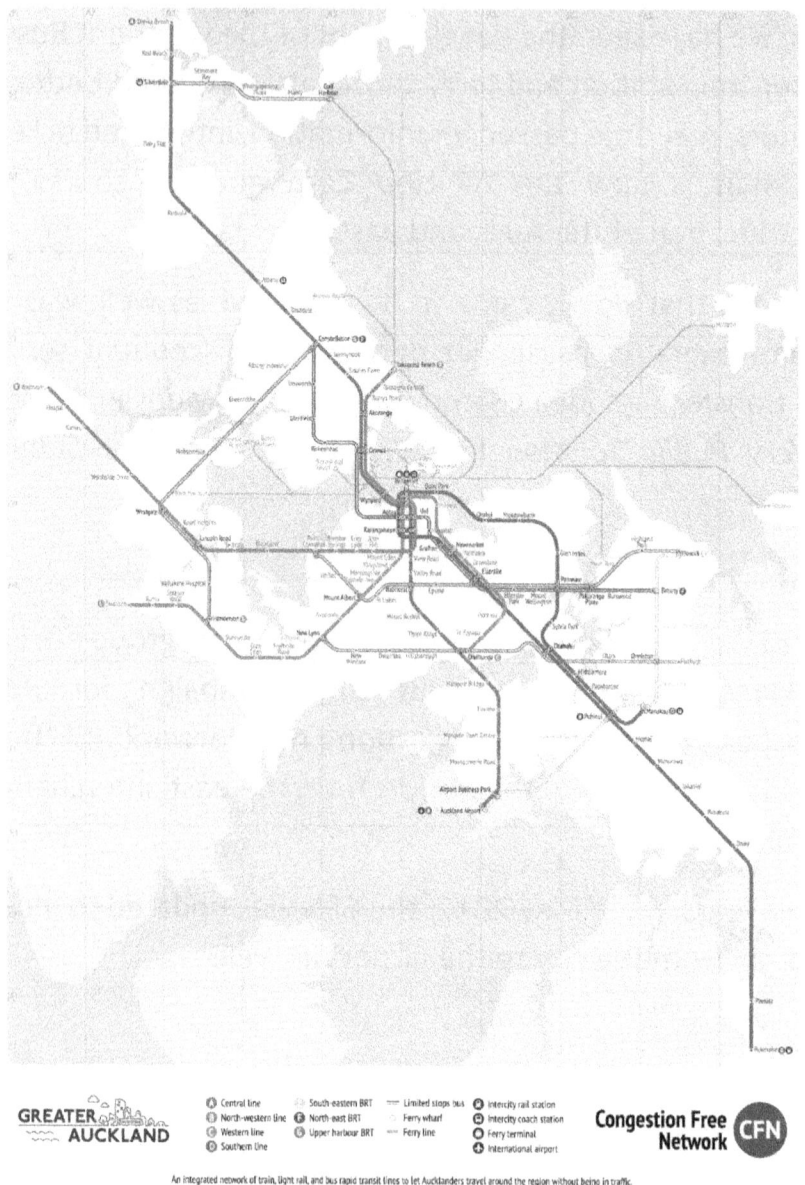

Reproduced under a link that says "Feel free to download, print, distribute, draw on, set alight, decorate your room, or re-blog," and with permission.

At that time, the Puhinui station was nothing special. It would obviously have to be upgraded.

Puhinui Train Station in 2008, looking southwards from the pedestrian overbridge. Photo by Ingolfson, 26 October, public domain image via Wikimedia Commons.

The real significance of Puhinui is that it made the airport accessible to a much larger region to the south of Auckland, which Greater Auckland also proposed to connect with a wider Regional Rapid Rail system.

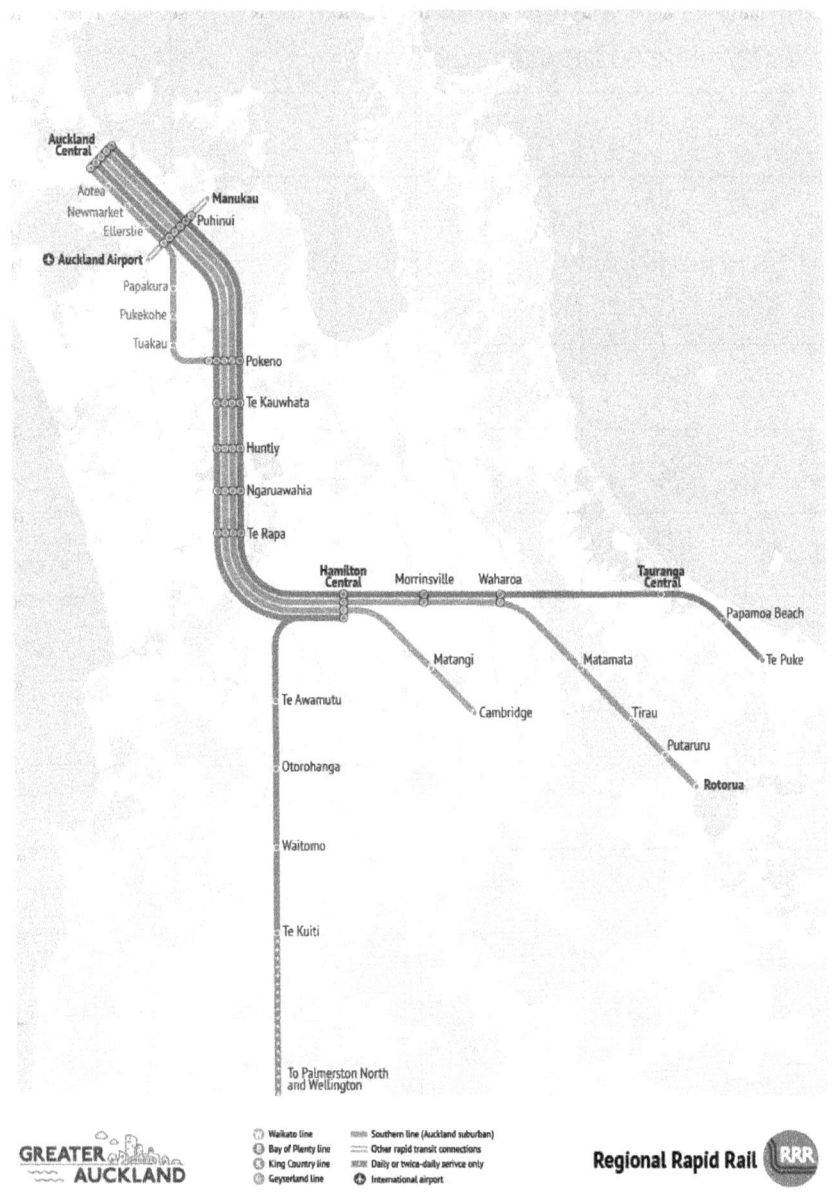

Reproduced with permission

Naming this area the 'Golden Triangle', Greater Auckland pointed out that it contained nearly half of New Zealand's population already, and that what was more, much of New Zealand's future growth was expected to occur within it.

Investment in an improved rail system would also create more opportunities and help to remedy the endemic poverty which besets much of the Golden Triangle region.

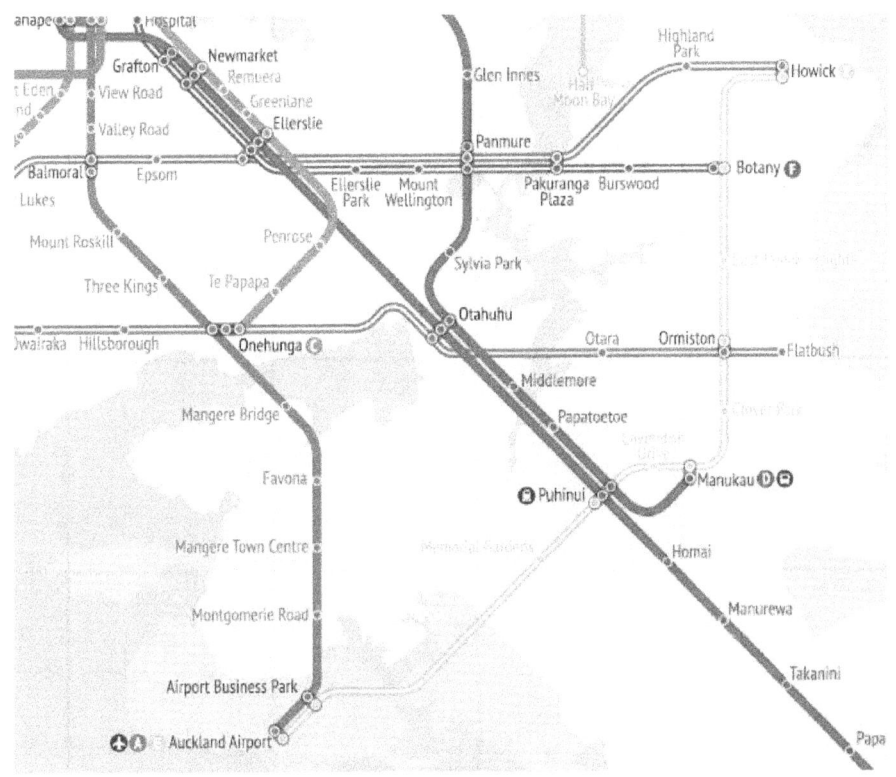

A zoomed-in detail from the CFN, including Puhinui and Auckland International Airport

Although Greater Auckland is an unofficial advocacy group, the New Zealand Government and Auckland Council had by this stage come to a similar long-term vision: much bolder than the position in 1999.

And so, they upgraded the Puhinui railway station into a major transport interchange, which opened in the middle of 2021.

The Puhinui Interchange as it is now. Photographs by Chris Harris.

The post-2021 Puhinui Interchange is really flash, with artwork inside that makes even the 2011-vintage Kingland station look rather utilitarian.

Photographed by Chris Harris, with the permission of Auckland One Rail

We are making progress all the time.

Getting back on track

Chapter 7

The Light Rail Saga

BY 2017, the Auckland Council favoured the reintroduction of trams to the innermost suburbs, which had had trams between 1902 and 1956.

In those days, the longest tram route was the one that ran from Queen Street to Onehunga. Others terminated at Avondale, or Mount Roskill, or Remuera.

Many cities overseas have reintroduced trams, generally in a 'modern' form, also known as light rail, which involves several carriages linked by a bendable joint, whereas in the old days each tram was rigid and separate.

Some cities, such as Melbourne, never got rid of the trams and merely went on to modernise them.

The main reason that trams were abolished in cities like Auckland was partly because of the cost of renewing the original tram-tracks, which were just then coming up for renewal after fifty or so years of faithful service.

But what really clinched the decision to abolish rather than renew was the fact that, running in the middle of the road as they did, to avoid parked cars (and in earlier times, carts), the older trams held up a growing volume of automobile traffic, which could not safely 'undertake' trams that had stopped to let passengers on and off.

Nor could they very easily overtake, as the trams boarded from the right as well, at least in those days. The streets sometimes had raised 'safety zones' in the very centre, for people to board and alight from the right.

Basically, the trams ruled the street, and motorists had to fit in as best they could.

Of course, these days, a technology that occupies the middle of the road, holding up and discouraging automobile traffic in the busiest parts of town would be seen as a good thing by the sorts of people who frequent pavement cafes and like to ride bicycles: this is one reason why trams have now come back into vogue.

And what this also tells us is that trams are, indeed, a technology that tends to go hand in hand with pavement cafes and streets that have plenty of pedestrian life and bicycles, whether we are speaking of the sorts of street scenes we see in some black and white movie from ages ago, or of the present day.

But the larger megalopolis needs more rapid forms of public transport as well. For which there is really only option that makes sense, namely, some sort of high-speed rail on a dedicated right-of-way.

This can then be integrated with more local tramways (and busways).

As we have seen, Greater Auckland's plan for a Congestion Free Network included the extension of the proposed Dominion Road tramway all the way through Onehunga and Mangere to the airport from May 2017 onwards.

In August 2017 the Labour Party, campaigning in the general election of that year, pledged to extend the Dominion Road tramway to the airport as well.

In hindsight this may well have been a mistake, because it introduced an element of complication to what was potentially otherwise a simple idea.

Laying surface light rail down Dominion Road as far as the SH 20 turnoff at Mount Roskill should have been fairly straightforward as, apparently, there are no water services down the middle of the road, which was a major tramway route from the earliest days and thus off limits for pipe-laying in that era.

But if the light rail was to run all the way to the airport, surface light rail on Dominion Road would probably have been too slow for airport passengers.

After nearly four years of investigations, a paper presented to the Cabinet in 2021, under the signature of Finance Minister Grant Robertson and Transport Minister Michael Wood, called

'Auckland Light Rail—Decision to Progress,' proposed three options, a surface light rail option estimated to cost $9 billion or $375 million per kilometre—a surprisingly high cost, which probably reflected the fact that it could not easily run in the middle of SH 20, which does not have broad medians—a tunnelled light metro along the lines of the London Underground, with low carriages and small tunnels costing $16.5 billion, and a partly tunnelled light rail system costing $14.6 billion, necessitating larger tunnels for stand-up carriages. The tunnels in the latter two options were to run beneath Dominion Road.

These figures were not firm but rather 'P50', meaning that there was a 50% chance they still could be wrong either way.

But wasn't Puhinui supposed to serve anyone who wanted to get to the airport quickly in any case?

Surely it would be possible to ditch light rail to the airport as impractical, and just go back to surface light rail down Dominion Road as far as Mount Roskill?

Well, yes: but the cabinet paper which presented the two light rail options and the light metro didn't mention the Puhinui Transport Interchange, which was just then being completed. Not once.

This interesting fact suggests that there may be something to a comment made by Mike Lee, in what is perhaps the best single critique of the airport tramway scheme, 'Auckland's

Light Rail Saga,' to the effect that much of the planning had been farmed out to a working group, eventually formed into a limited liability company, that had come to see itself as a competitor to the existing heavy rail system.

A competitor heavily reliant on publicly funded investment in improbably lengthy suburban tunnels, and not as a short-range surface-running complement to the heavy rail system:

Apart from the single line to the airport, Auckland Light Rail Ltd wanted to build light rail to the North Shore, to the Northwest, and even to run light rail in competition with trains down the future Avondale to Southdown rail corridor.

The ambition, no less, was to build a parallel passenger rail system in Auckland, with separate rolling stock, different gauge lines, catenary, signalling, etc., to, in effect, duplicate the heavy rail system for which the ratepayers and taxpayers of Auckland have already invested so dearly.

This impression would only be reinforced when, a bit over three months after the publication of Lee's 'Saga', the Labour Government announced its $45 billion harbour crossing plan, which included a 21-km long light rail tunnel from the downtown to Albany, though most of the cost was to be incurred in the form of road tunnels (thereby adding to CBD congestion, but that is another matter).

After allowing for inflation, $45 billion in today's New Zealand money is what the British and the French spent to develop

Concorde in the 1960s. It is also about what the development of the atomic bomb cost the Americans in World War II.

But to paraphrase the old Jim Beam ad — this wasn't Concorde. Nor the Manhattan Project.

It was just a local scheme that would have left no money at all for the Golden Triangle, Auckland's true growth frontier.

And probably not much money for anything else, truth be told. The cost of Concorde was spread over more than 100 million British and French people at the time, the Manhattan Project over some 140 million WW2-era Americans, whereas there are only just over 1.7 million Aucklanders right now.

The irony in all this is that the revival of the light rail idea in Auckland, between 2015 and 2023, was originally intended to be sensible, doable, practical and affordable in ways that would improve local streetscapes and generally bring Auckland up to the standard of other cities that have put in modern trams, and never regretted doing so.

Instead, it turned into a monstrous deka-billion octopus, its tentacles a series of improbably long suburban tunnels, into which the incoming government felt impelled to plant an exploding harpoon.

Predictably, the coalition government elected in October 2023 scrapped both the airport light rail scheme and the $45 billion harbour crossing scheme.

The Government has proposed 'trackless trams', meaning longer-than-usual bendy buses with a degree of guidance. However, this is no quick and easy solution. It requires significant road reconstruction in its own right, as the road surface may otherwise become rutted by buses running along the exact same path, and also because long, articulated vehicles will work best in the centre of the road anyway, in ways that necessitate significant changes to the road.

There is still hope for surface light rail in Auckland. The mayor, Wayne Brown, continues to support the idea.

Plus, there are a host of emerging modern track and vehicle technologies that will allow tram tracks to be laid more easily and quickly, with only 300mm deep excavation in the road surface and the rapid laying of track, instead of 600mm deep with slow and laborious construction, which has been the norm from the 1800s until now.

A good example is the LR55 track system by Professor Lewis Lesley, author of *The Light Rail Developer's Handbook* and now principal at Trampower Ltd, who has prepared a custom proposal for Dominion Road (available from the authors at admin [at] a-maverick dot com and potentially soon online).

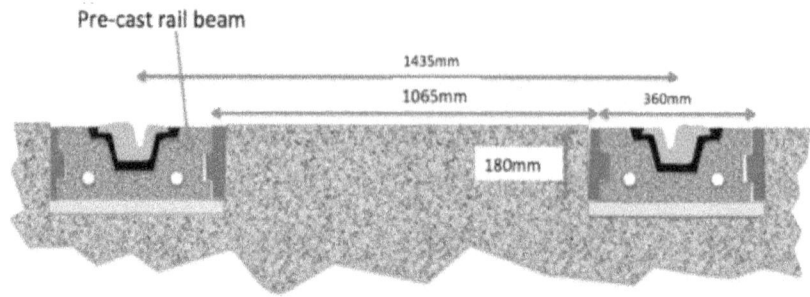

LR55 precast beams including steel tracks on rubber bonding (black), laid in two milled slots in the roadway. Courtesy of Trampower Ltd.

Unless we are mistaken, this kind of technology does not seem to have been canvassed by Auckland Light Rail. If so, as with the enduring myth of an Auckland too sprawling for public transport to have been effective, this is perhaps another instance of the price we pay for a lack of diverse sources of expertise and criticism on our little islands.

Otherwise, these new technologies suggest that with reduced disruption, and still more so with reduced cost as compared to the ALR proposals, it should be possible to renew Auckland's surface-running tramways without too much difficulty in the near future.

So, watch this space!

(PS: for more on what happened to the original plan, and what seems like the suppression of the fact that it was shovel-ready in 2018, see Conor Sharp's 14 October 2024 post 'Who benefits from secrecy around public infrastructure?,' on the Greater Auckland website.)

Conclusion: No More Missed Chances?

WHAT stands out, in the end, is that we don't seem to take Auckland seriously, or to look at the city as a positive national asset. As a result, we keep missing our chances to make it better.

Everything to do with Auckland is denied, begrudged, or too little and too late.

Whenever pundits and politicians talk about farming as the backbone of New Zealand, they seem to forget that Auckland exists.

Others express pessimism about Auckland's future.

Wouldn't it be remarkable if our politicians leaned into a vision for Auckland's future that came with some real positivity?

There is one big gleam of hope on the horizon, and that is that with the falling costs of renewable energy, New Zealand, which has an abundance of wind, water, sunshine, and geothermal heat, might be able to offer itself as a platform for new industries, in ways that would mop up urban unemployment and underemployment and provide the funds needed for all the infrastructure we have neglected.

Conclusion

At any rate, there is little reason to suppose that Auckland will stop growing. So, we might as well have a national conversation about how we can make it both big and beautiful.

As we look ahead, we should be thinking of a 'Green New Deal' and the opportunities that it can offer to revitalise the city and to lend us some optimism about its future.